Marjorie McCa...

Siames...

Everything About Acquisition, Care,
Nutrition, Behavior, and Health

Full-color Photographs
Illustrations by Michele Earle-Bridges

BARRON'S

ENTS

WHAT IS A SIAMESE?

The exotic Siamese is both beautiful and fascinating. A loving and active companion, this breed is colorful both in looks and personality. The distinct colorpoint pattern of the Siamese easily makes it one of the more popular and recognizable breeds in the world.

Origins

Believed to be one of the oldest cat breeds, the sleek Siamese is said to have originally come from Thailand. This ancient Asian land, once known as Siam, is the source of the breed's name and its more flattering, legendary reference, "The Royal Cats of Siam." The Western world first became acquainted with Siamese cats around the late 1880s, when they were imported into England and began appearing in cat shows there. Since those early days, the breed's popularity has soared among cat fanciers worldwide. The breed also has genetically influenced many other breeds, including the Oriental, the Balinese, the Javanese, the Himalayan, and the Tonkinese.

While the Siamese's striking color contrast is its most prominent feature, its head shape and body structure are equally distinct. The breed standard established by the Cat Fanciers' Association (CFA), the world's largest registry of pedigreed cats, calls for a long, lithe body topped by a tapering wedge-shaped head, triangular in appearance and offset by large, pointed ears. The cat is svelte but muscular. The legs are long and slim, higher in the hind end than in the front. The tail is long, thin, and tapering to a fine point, with no kinks. The eyes are almond-shaped, but never crossed.

While the wedge-shaped head tends to dominate show rings today, many people still prefer the rounder look of the "Apple-head" or traditional Siamese. Regardless of your preference, the Siamese makes a loving and lively feline companion.

Siamese Characteristics

To me, all cats are beautiful, but Siamese hold a special attraction. Part of this attraction

Siamese make excellent companions to children and adults.

comes from their unusual coat pattern and coloring, but the greater part is their personality. Let us look first at the coat, which is much easier to describe than their complex and marvelous personality.

Coat Pattern

The Siamese coat pattern consists of darker coloring on the "points" (face, ears, feet, and tail) and a much lighter tint on the neck and body, producing a dramatic contrast of light and dark. This is called the pointed or Himalayan pattern.

Coat Colors

The basic Siamese colors are seal point, chocolate point, blue point, and lilac point. The seal point is the darkest, with the points appearing seal brown to black. The chocolate point has brown points, ranging from bittersweet chocolate brown to pale milk chocolate. The blue point has slate-gray points, and the lilac point, silvery lavender points. In each case the body color should be a very pale tint of the point color. Other point colors have been brought into the Siamese breed by crossing it with domestic shorthair cats. As a result, there are now cats with every imaginable point coloration, including tortie (tortoiseshell) point, red point, lynx point (stripes on the points), and cream point. Some of these are recognized separately as Colorpoint Shorthairs, depending on the registry.

Eye Color

Another startling feature of the Siamese is its blue eyes, also a result of the gene responsible for the coat pattern. The shade of blue ranges from a pale china-blue to a deep blue-violet.

✔ The color is a result of a reduced amount of pigment in the iris, caused by the partial albinism of the genotype, the scattering of light by the colloidal substance within the eye, and the reflection of light from the retina.

✔ The seal points tend to have the deepest shades of blue and the lilac point the lightest.

✔ The eyes are almond-shaped, and should not be crossed.

Body Type

Today's Siamese comes in two basic body types generally referred to as Extreme and Traditional. The Extreme body type is the svelte, elegant Siamese with the wedge-shaped head and long tapering lines. Judging from its prevalence, this look is favored in the show ring today.

The Traditional Siamese, also known as the Apple-head, has a rounder, heavier body type, and is a larger cat overall. This look has its devoted followers, too, and proponents of this version claim that it is truer to what the original Siamese looked like, before breeders began selectively breeding for more refined characteristics and ultimately altering the body type.

Breeders of the Extreme Siamese type disagree, however, claiming that their version is closer to the original. As proof, they point to centuries-old drawings of early cats with slim bodies and pale-colored coats sporting dark points. They believe this early, original look was later influenced—corrupted, some would say—by cross matings with other breeds.

Regardless of who is right on this issue, the Siamese is a lovely and lovable cat. Basically, it all boils down to whether you prefer the slender Extreme look or the larger Traditional cats. The nice thing is, you have a choice; but whichever version you choose, you still have a Siamese with its exotic coloring and its endearing and energetic personality.

Personality

The Siamese personality is as varied and individual as that of cats in general, but there are some traits that are particularly evident in Siamese. They are generally active and energetic. The most endearing and common trait of the properly reared Siamese is their attachment to their humans. They want to be, at the very least, in the same room with their person. How close to their person can vary from time to time and cat to cat, but most will seek close contact often, particularly when their person settles in a chair or a bed. Experienced Siamese watchers long ago discovered that there are lap Siamese and shoulder Siamese, a distinction that seems to be hereditary.

Voice

Another special trait of the Siamese personality is their voice and how they use it. The voice itself is very different from non-Siamese breeds; it is usually louder and much more variable in tone and pitch. They have been mistaken for crying babies, but don't let that put you off. That intensity of vocalization will not be prolonged if you are smart enough to understand what dire need must be attended to by you. Most of the time they talk at a conversational level, and many seem to enjoy spoken exchanges with their humans. Their vocabulary can be quite extensive, much beyond "mew" and "meow." As with all generalizations, there are exceptions. We had with us a handsome and exceptionally sweet chocolate-point male, whom we had leased for a couple of years. Although he had an illustrious name, we called him Mou because that's the only word he spoke. No matter what the message—"Scratch my chin, please."; "Feed me!"; "Hello, you beautiful lilac-point girl."—the word was always "mou."

Human Interaction

Siamese will follow you around the house, go for walks with you, if permitted, and play games with you, traits that they share with the dog family. Unlike most dogs, however, they may subject you to a probationary period before giving you their total trust. Observing the rules of Siamese etiquette (see "Understanding Siamese," page 34) will make for a speedy acceptance and a lasting bond of affection.

Intelligence

And last, but not least, is their intelligence. They are smart and sensitive, particularly to their humans. They are not dumb, incapable of learning, nor inscrutable, as one often hears, especially in comparison to dogs, pigs, and horses. They are feline, and if a person has no understanding of feline nature, he or she may come to those terribly mistaken conclusions. Part of the joy of living with Siamese is learning from them about feline nature and about their individual personalities, for no two Siamese are identical.

In a Nutshell

So, if the image of a sleek, graceful, blue-eyed, communicative, responsive, and loving feline companion appeals to you, the Siamese is your cat. If you do not already have a Siamese, the next chapter will help you find one.

ACQUISITION

Once you've decided that you want to own a Siamese, there's a lot you need to know about finding the right breeder and a healthy cat or kitten. Resist the temptation to purchase a kitten on impulse.

First Steps

The hardest part about getting your Siamese cat or kitten is patience. It is very hard to resist the temptation to just go out, find a Siamese, and take it home. But think of your long-term goal—a long, happy relationship. This calls for thoughtful preparation.

Examine Your Commitment

First, be certain that you are ready, that you understand the responsibilities involved, and that you are prepared to make a commitment to love and care for the cat for its lifetime—which in Siamese may be 20 years. What is "ready"? A young woman once came to me for a kitten. She seemed very mature, financially able, and very eager to share her life with the kitten. She called frequently, both while waiting for the time to pick up her kitten and afterward to tell me how happy she was with it. But

Most people prefer to acquire a kitten, but getting an adult cat has advantages, especially if it has already been vaccinated and spayed or neutered.

before a year passed, she asked me to take back the cat, an adult now, as her new boyfriend was jealous of it. Obviously, this person had not been ready. (Fortunately, a friend of a friend was ready, adopted the cat, and has made a happy and secure home for it ever since.)

Kittens and Cats

Another point to remember is that kittenhood is not permanent. As in humans, babies are appealing and very playful, but adults are quieter and may be thought less "cute." Adult Siamese continue to play, but not as much as kittens. Of course, as in humans, adults have more understanding, are more sophisticated, and form deeper and more complex relationships than kittens. If this is not what you want, do not get a Siamese or any other kitten or cat.

A final admonition: Illness will occur even with the best of care. If you would hesitate to take an ailing cat to the veterinarian or would become angry at a cat for throwing up or having diarrhea, please do not get a Siamese or any other cat.

Finding the Right Veterinarian

If you now find yourself ready to begin a long, happy relationship with a Siamese, the next step is to find a suitable veterinarian. Recommendations from friends can be helpful, but there are certain things you should investigate for yourself, as you would in finding a personal physician. The most obvious consideration is location; the veterinarian should be close enough to your home so that travel is not a serious problem. In some areas, you may find a veterinarian with a mobile practice who makes house calls. Ideally, the veterinarian's practice is limited to cats, but even in large cities there are few in this category. There are many small-animal veterinarians who treat a sizable number of cats, stay abreast of new findings in feline care, and are aware of the very real physiological differences between cats and dogs. A veterinarian who meets these criteria is a very good candidate for "suitable veterinarian."

If you live in a rural area and only large-animal veterinarians are nearby, do not despair. Just be willing to ask the veterinarian to confer with feline practitioners or to take your Siamese to a veterinary school or major animal hospital for other than routine care. In any case, you should interview prospective veterinarians before getting your Siamese. In the interview try to determine whether the veterinarian will be willing to take time to explain procedures and conditions to you and whether he or she will be open to suggestions or comments from others, particularly if they do not see many Siamese. After all, you must bear the ultimate responsibility for your pet's health; to make sound decisions for your pet, you need to be an active partner with your veterinarian, not an unquestioning client. The suitable veterinarian will not feel threatened by such an attitude, but will welcome a client who wants to learn and to make informed decisions for the pet.

Finding a Siamese

Sources

Now comes the most exciting part—finding the kitten or cat. Again, you may be fortunate in having leads from friends who have Siamese. If not, check the classified advertisements in newspapers and breeders' advertisements in cat magazines, visit cat shows, and call the major cat registries for breeders in your area (see Information). These sources should yield a first contact with a reputable breeder or dealer. By definition, reputable breeders and dealers are known by and have connections with other breeders and dealers and, if they do not have the Siamese for you, will direct you to others.

Before you contact the breeder or dealer, prepare yourself with a list of questions and be prepared to answer certain questions yourself. You will be seeking assurance that this is indeed a reputable source, and the reputable source will be trying to assess your ability to provide a good home for his or her cherished baby.

If you are new to Siamese, you really need the support of someone with many years' experience. The best way to gain such support is by buying a cat or kitten from a knowledgeable individual; therefore, your first questions should ask how much experience the breeder or dealer has and whether continued contact and questions from clients, particularly those with their first Siamese, would be welcomed.

CHECKLIST

Self-Test

The following questions will help you decide if you are ready to have a Siamese. If you answer no to three or more questions, there are too many strikes against the likelihood of a long and happy Siamese-person relationship and you should either delay getting a cat or get a different sort of pet.

1 Will I be upset by the inevitable wear and tear on my household goods—the scratch on the piano bench, the pulled thread on the sofa, the broken cup?

2 If there are other members of the household, do they agree to having a cat?

3 If there is a landlord, does he or she allow pets?

4 If there are children in the household, will I make certain that they learn how to treat a cat and make sure it is not abused?

5 Will my Siamese have companionship (a person or another pet) most of the time?

6 Am I willing to say home weekends until it is adjusted to its new home?

7 When I leave the cat for a time, will I be able to get a friend, neighbor, or professional catsitter to care for it?

8 Can I deal with cleaning up after a sick cat (which is likely to include diarrhea and vomiting), and with nursing it (which may include cleaning wounds and giving medication)?

9 Am I aware that kittenhood is very short, and am I looking forward to adulthood of my Siamese?

10 Can I afford the cost of cat food, *not table scraps*, which may be $20 or more per month, and of veterinary care, which may average $200 or more per year?

11 Am I or any members of my household allergic to cats?

Cost

Pet, Breeder, or Show

Another question, of course, must be about price. Most breeders will have three categories: pet, breeder, and show quality.

Pet quality: The pet-quality kitten or cat has one or more traits, such as crossed eyes or a kinked tail, that make it undesirable for breeding and unqualified for showing; this will be the lowest-priced category. A breeder usually stipulates that these cats be altered. If you are not interested in breeding or showing and have no objection yourself to the undesirable trait, include them in your search.

Breeder quality: Breeder-quality Siamese are showable; that is, they have no traits that would disqualify them, but they are deemed by the breeder as not likely to go far in shows because of less serious flaws, such as ears too small or set too high on the head, eyes too round, tail a bit too short for the length of the body, and so on. Many of this quality are sold as pets with an agreement to alter.

Kittens are adorable, but before you acquire one, make sure you are able and prepared to care for it for the rest of its life, which may be as long as two decades or more.

area to another. Kittens older than six months and adults usually cost less. A breeder may even have an adult for adoption. Perhaps this is the time to put in a word for considering adults as well as kittens. Adult Siamese are capable of adjusting to new homes at any age, so long as they are properly cared for. This case is typical: A kitten was bought by a woman to be the companion of her invalid husband. The kitten was his constant companion until the man's death, about one year later. The distraught widow could not bear the sight of the cat, which reminded her of her husband, and after several weeks of keeping the cat shut in a room by himself returned the bewildered cat to his breeder. The breeder found a home for the cat with a young couple with small children and dogs. The cat bonded to the new family, despite the many differences in lifestyle from his first and second homes, and lived very happily to an old age.

Show quality: Show-quality Siamese will be the most expensive and may be subdivided into "show" and "top show." Show quality should come with a guarantee that the cat has no traits that would prevent it from achieving championship. Top show kittens conform so closely to the Siamese breed standard that they are likely to achieve top wins in shows and national recognition. Do not expect to buy a top show kitten; they are rarely produced, even by top show parents, and are usually kept by the breeder or are offered at top prices to other established breeders and exhibitors. In fact, a breeder who offers to sell a top show kitten to a newcomer should be very closely scrutinized or probably crossed off the list altogether.

Condition

Health

You should also ask about the health of the kitten or cat and its line (a breeder's term for forebears), including whether there are any congenital problems or predispositions to conditions such as cardiomyopathy (disorder of the heart muscle). A more tactful approach might be to ask about the longevity of its relatives, particularly of its grandparents and older siblings.

Age

The prices for kittens range from a few hundred dollars for pet quality to thousands of dollars for top show quality, and vary from one

Whether you're adopting or purchasing a Siamese, expect the seller to ask you questions related to your ability to care for the cat.

Immunizations

The breeder or dealer should be able to assure you that all of the adults and ready-to-go kittens in his or her care have been vaccinated against rhinotracheitis, feline panleukopenia, and calici virus, the so-called three-in-one vaccination. Some sources also immunize against chlamydia, but it is not given as early as the three-in-one. The adults in the cattery should be immunized against feline leukemia virus, or have certificates of negative leukemia test results dated within the past three months. Many breeders and dealers do not give leukemia vaccine to the kittens that are to be sold, preferring to leave that to the new owner.

Guarantees

Finally, you should ask about guarantees of health and personality. Of course, no one can make absolute guarantees of anything, but

This kitten is still too young to go to a new home. Most breeders release them only after they are at least 12 weeks old.

reputable sources will have some arrangement to deal with a buyer's dissatisfaction. Some sources insist that the buyer take the cat or kitten to the buyer's veterinarian immediately for an examination. If there is a personality problem, reputable breeders will give a refund for the return of the Siamese within a certain period of time if it is in good health. Beyond those specifications the breeder may not choose to give a refund, but will surely accept return of the cat or kitten.

The Process of Selection

The Seller's Questions

If you decide to purchase your Siamese from a breeder, he or she will have questions for you. These will be aimed at determining whether you will provide a good home and security for a Siamese. Expect to be asked if you have had a Siamese before; if the answer is no, if you have had other cats before; if so, what became of them; whether you intend to keep the cat indoors; if you want it only as a pet or for breeding and showing; and what you would do if you found that you could no longer keep it.

The First Visit

After this first contact, if both sides are agreeable, you are ready to visit the breeder and see the Siamese. If you are buying a kitten, the chances that there are kittens available and old enough to go are slim. Here is where more patience is called for. Ideally, Siamese kittens should be at least 12 weeks old and have had at least two rounds of recommended vaccinations before going to a new home. Reasons will be given in a later chapter, but it is basically a matter of weaning time and development of the immune system. Most breeders will allow quiet visitors to see kittens once they are about five or six weeks old. It may be possible to make a deposit and reserve your kitten then, if you wish.

The Clean Kitten

When you handle the kitten, be alert to signs of flea and ear mite infestation. Fleas may be seen in the short, light fur of a kitten. If not, ruffle its fur backward along its back and look for small, black flecks; these are flea feces and a sure sign that fleas are around. Look into the ears. Excessive amounts of ear wax, which in cats is normally brown, coating the inside of the ear or clumped in the folds, could mean ear mite infestation. If the ears are clean, but look irritated—redder than the skin elsewhere, for example—or the kitten scratches its ears or shakes its head, it may have just undergone an ear cleaning or treatment for mites.

The Healthy Kitten

Judging the health and condition of the Siamese is very easy if you keep in mind the images of the two extremes—a cat in top condition and one that is ill. The ailing cat or kitten will look like a bundle of misery. Its coat is "open" (not sleek), dull, and unkempt. Instead of lying like a sphinx, it keeps its forefeet back and to the sides of its chest, so that its elbows stick up. Its eyes have partly raised third eyelids or "haws." The eyes and nose may be runny or encrusted. The ill cat may also have a bad odor. When held, it has a slack feeling, and when stretched out, it may be bony along the back and swollen in the belly. The happier image is the healthy Siamese. Its coat is clean, sweet smelling, shiny, and down flat, giving a painted-on look. (A kitten's coat may be fluffy for a time.) When reclining, it looks at ease and comfortable. It is alert and responsive. Its eyes are bright and clear, with no haws showing. When held, it feels firm and taut, even as a young kitten. When stretched out, its body is tubular (unless it has just had a meal) and firm; individual vertebrae are not felt as you run a hand down the spine.

Personality

Judging the personality of the cat or kitten is really a matter of determining how it was treated from birth and whether you feel an initial attraction to it. If it had close, loving contact with humans from the beginning and weaning was not begun before six weeks, the chances are very high that it will be a loving adult with a healthy Siamese personality. How it responds to you will depend upon how you behave toward it. If you have not had much experience with felines, it would be a good idea to follow the example of the breeder in approaching and making contact with the Siamese. Common sense tells you that you must not appear threatening or loud; so walk and speak softly and make yourself as small as possible as you approach them. Do not expect young kittens to be very interested in humans; from about four to fourteen weeks it is normal for them to be more interested in playing, especially with each other, than anything else.

The Final Decision

If all is to your liking, expect to visit with the breeder and the cat or kitten for at least an hour. By then, you and the breeder will have asked all the questions, have some knowledge of each other, and can tell whether the Siamese in question should go to you. If the decision is yes, your search is over and your life is about to take on a whole new dimension. If no, keep looking; patience and determination will get you to your Siamese.

Conclusion

Accompaniments to Purchase

When you do find your Siamese and are ready to take it home, the breeder or dealer

---

=== TIP ===

Visiting the Cattery
✔ When you visit the cattery or pet shop, look at more than the cats and kittens.
✔ The place should be clean, but not like an operating room.
✔ There should be no strong odors of uncleaned litter pans or of spoiled food.
✔ The water bowls should be full and clean.
✔ There should be beds in warm places and toys.
✔ There should be evidence of much human contact.

---

will give you its health records, including dates and kinds of vaccinations, its pedigree, even if you want it only as a pet, and its registration papers. These last may not be given if you are getting a pet-quality kitten, or they may be given if marked "to be altered." The breeder will probably give you all the advice you need about its care and feeding. Some even have printed instructions for new owners! Be sure to exchange telephone numbers and get permission to call back for further advice and consultation, if needed.

Going Home

At last the happy moment has arrived and you are taking your Siamese to its new home, which you have prepared as described in the next chapter.

The first days together should be planned for well in advance of the day the new kitten or cat arrives. Thorough mental and physical preparations will prevent or ease many problems that are common during the adjustment period.

Mental Preparation

By the time the decision to get a Siamese is made, much of the mental preparation has been done. The idea of sharing space and leisure time with a cat is obvious and usually comes to mind first. Perhaps less obvious is the extent and range of interaction between human and Siamese that is likely to occur. And finally, least obvious, is the realization and acceptance of the responsibility for many years, we hope, of care.

Even with the most careful preparations by all concerned, the move to a new home can be scary for a Siamese. There is no way to predict how the new kitten or cat will react. Even littermates can have quite different personalities and very different responses. Be prepared

Decide from the outset if your Siamese is going to be an indoor or an outdoor cat. Cats kept indoors live longer, healthier lives, while cats allowed outside are exposed to many hazards.

for anything from the terror-stricken invisible kitten under the sofa to the instantly-at-ease, take-charge Major Cat.

Physical Preparation

The physical things that can be done in advance can be categorized as: 1. household insurance, 2. Siamese insurance, 3. necessities, and 4. luxuries.

Household Insurance

Household insurance begins with moving small, fragile objects out of harm's way. Stand in the middle of each room and gaze around the entire room. Imagine a small, furry creature running, skidding, and jumping on and over every surface, and secure anything that could be endangered. Remember, a kitten has more energy and less muscular control than an adult and has yet to learn how high it cannot jump. The soil of large potted plants should be covered with netting or otherwise made inaccessible to little feet. For a kitten, floor-length lace curtains are magnets, so loop them up or put them away until the little one grows up.

Siamese Insurance

Siamese insurance means making your home safe for your feline companion. Access to dangerous places must be blocked off. For a kitten, this includes narrow openings such as under the stove or alongside the refrigerator. Check the areas where pipes go through walls or floors and seal any gaps. Cover open sump pumps. For kittens and cats, windows that are opened must have full-length screens. High-rise balconies should have screen doors. Screening must be strong and sturdy, as cats can claw through them and fall or escape. Household cleaning solutions or air fresheners that contain formaldehyde or phenol must be outlawed. Poisonous houseplants must be banished or suspended out of reach (for a partial list of poisonous plants, see page 47).

Necessities. Beds, litter boxes, food and water dishes, and grooming supplies.

The Necessities

The necessities are one or more litter pans, depending upon the size of your home and the youthfulness of your Siamese, a water bowl, and a bed.

Litter pans: These come in a variety of styles. Keep it simple and very accessible to start with—a plain pan several inches deep and big enough to allow the cat or kitten plenty of elbow room. Place the pan where the cat can get to it easily. Do not expect any cat to be happy with a litter pan in the basement of a three-story house. If your new Siamese is a young kitten and your house is a spread-out ranch-style or multistoried home, provide two or more pans until the kitten reaches adulthood. Later, if you want to try fancier arrangements, such as covered pans, do so after the cat is well adjusted to its new home. Get either the same litter the breeder uses or the basic unscented clay granules and put it in the pan to a depth of about 2 inches (5.1 cm). A slotted scoop completes the toilet setup.

Food and water: Select a location for the food and water station. It should be out of the way but easy to get to. The water bowl should be of glass or ceramic material intended for such use. Some plastics have been found to be unsuitable water bowls because potentially harmful compounds leach out of the plastic into the water. Dishes for canned food should be flat. Bowls may be used for dry food. An easily cleaned mat of some sort under the food and water dishes is helpful, as some Siamese are messy eaters, either dragging their food out of the dish before eating it or not eating their crunchies over the bowl.

Beds: There are all sorts of beds for cats; follow your fancy. The only rules are: 1. they

Cat furniture and toys, including scratching posts and a cat tree.

should be appealing to the cat, and 2. they should be washable. To be appealing to the user, they need to be soft and warm. Most Siamese enjoy what I call the doughnut bed. These are simply made and machine washable. Another favorite looks like a wheeless covered wagon in soft sculpture with its top supported with arches of corset stays. Do not be surprised, however, if your special Siamese buddy abandons his bed when you get into yours and wants to share your pillow or to snuggle under the covers by your knees.

Luxuries

Last, but not least, we come to the luxuries—toys, scratching posts, trees, window perches, and the like. (Your Siamese will rank these as necessities, of course.) The rule for toys is fun but not dangerous. Examine toys just as you would for human babies. There should be no hard parts that could come off and be swallowed or lodge in the throat. Then, there are special feline dangers. Loose string, yarn, rubber bands, and ribbon can be fatal. While cats can vomit readily, they have great difficulty spitting out long, flexible material, in part because the barbs on the tongue are directed toward the back of the mouth. Once a long, stringy object gets partway down the throat, they cannot rid themselves of it. In the stomach, it may not be bulky enough to cause vomiting and will pass on into the intestine. If these problems are not corrected quickly, a very painful death can result.

Scratching posts: Some sort of scratching material really is a necessity, not a luxury. One can get by with the simplest sort, such as a scrap of carpet, or get very fancy with scratching posts and cat trees. Again, the first rule is that of cat-approval. The texture of the carpet should be such that they can really get their claws in and find strong resistance. A low, tight, nubby weave or the jute back of carpeting is very popular among my Siamese. The next consideration is placement. While they are small, a piece of scratching material on the floor is fine, but as they get bigger, they want to stretch upward as they scratch. A piece of carpet can be attached directly to the wall or to a board that is set at an angle on a base or around a post set in a base. The height should be slightly more than the cat's greatest reach.

Window perches: Sitting in windows is a major occupation for Siamese when their people are out of the house. If the windowsills in your home are not wide enough to allow your cat to rest and observe the outside world, a window perch would solve the problem. This is

Cats will often share a litter box, but it's best to provide one box for each cat.

basically carpeted or cloth-covered shelves that are propped on the windowsill.

Cat tree: The ultimate in luxury is the cat tree, which provides places for scratching, exercise, rest, seclusion, and that most important Siamese duty—supervision of its realm. The tree should be freestanding, not the tension-pole type, and substantial, so that flying leaps do not cause the slightest movement. They must be tip-proof and stable. Cats shy away from things that give way under them. Again, the height is critical. If you want the Siamese on its furniture and not on yours, be sure its tree is taller than your furniture.

The typical Siamese color pattern features darker colored "points" on the ears, face (called the mask), paws, and tail.

The slight receding chin, smaller ears, and shorter tail of this seal lynx point are the result of the non-Siamese component in its heritage.

Most kittens love to play peek-a-boo under a cover or in a paper bag. But don't let them play with plastic bags.

(A Siamese would lie on a bed of nails if it were the topmost thing around!) At least one company that I know of allows the customer to design the tree, choosing the placement of perches, tunnels, and houses, the overall height, and the color and type of carpeting.

Cat carrier: Stock up on food and litter, and if you do not already have one, get a cat carrier. A cardboard box with holes punched in it will *not* do. Being enclosed and unable to see out could terrify the cat or kitten, which is bad enough, but a panic-stricken Siamese can tear out of a cardboard box and escape.

This inquisitive young seal point exemplifies the so-called Apple-head, which is pet quality. This look is still preferred by many. There are no distinct differences in personality between show and pet quality Siamese.

At last the day arrives, and you bring home your Siamese. What you do with it after you get in the front door depends on the state of the cat's nerves and the circumstances in your home.

✔ Consider first of all the most reassuring and safest things to do for the cat. At best, whether a cat or kitten, it will be nervous from the trip. Do not be in a hurry to let it out of the carrier.

✔ Have the household as quiet as possible. If there are other pets, put them in another room. Everyone should walk and talk quietly.

✔ Small children should not be allowed to rush at the cat or scream at it, even while it is still in the carrier.

✔ Whether the Siamese seems calm or nervous, the best idea is to take it to a bedroom or another room that can be closed off before letting it out. One strange room is much less frightening to the Siamese than a whole houseful of new, uncharted territory. An adjoining bathroom could contain its litter box and water bowl. When the Siamese begins to feel at home in the room and with you—it may be in five minutes or three days—introduce it to the rest of the house.

Other Pets

If there are other dogs or other cats already in the home, careful introductions will be needed. Be prepared for the worst—they try to kill each other—and hope for the best—buddies at first sight. First allow the pets to see and smell each other with a barrier between them. This can be achieved by putting the new cat in a cage or its carrier and allowing the older pet to come over and get acquainted. The bars or grill not only prevent fights but give both of them a sense of security. If the first pet is an adult cat and the new Siamese is a kitten, the adult will still probably hiss and swat at the newcomer (in a cat's mind anything new, no matter how small, could be a terrible monster), but will accept it more quickly than if the second cat is also an adult. Do not leave them free in the house together until you are sure there is, at least, a truce. Most do become friends, either immediately or, more usually, after a few weeks.

Children

To avoid any mishaps, supervise all contact between cats and kids. Because squeals and screams will likely frighten the cat and make it fearful of children, instruct your children to be quiet and

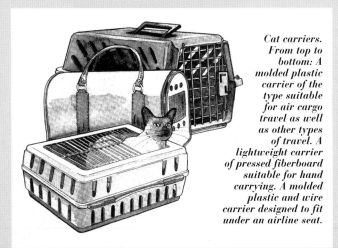

Cat carriers. From top to bottom: A molded plastic carrier of the type suitable for air cargo travel as well as other types of travel. A lightweight carrier of pressed fiberboard suitable for hand carrying. A molded plastic and wire carrier designed to fit under an airline seat.

respectful around kitty. Teach your children how to hold and handle a cat properly. Show them how and where to pet the cat safely (underbellies are off limits), and explain that ears and tails are not handles to be pulled.

Kittens are especially fragile and can be easily injured if dropped or handled carelessly. A child's unintentional roughness may also result in the child being bitten or scratched, if the cat becomes frightened and feels the need to defend itself. This certainly won't set their relationship off to a good start or help the cat feel at ease in its new home.

First Reaction

Even with the smoothest possible transition, the Siamese may not want to eat for the first day or two in its new home. Do not be disturbed unless there are other signs of illness. Put out food and water, of course, and be patient. If you want to try harder, put a dollop of warm, strained baby food chicken or turkey on your finger and offer it to the starveling. If that succeeds, next put a dollop of baby food on top of the regular food.

Adjustment

Whatever the circumstances, the adjustment period will go much faster and more smoothly if the Siamese has maximum contact with its new family. For this reason, most people arrange the homecoming for just before the weekend or a holiday.

Make sure everyone in the household knows the proper way to hold a kitten or cat. The paws are controlled and the weight is supported.

As the Siamese begins to move freely around its new home there are bound to be transgressions; after all, it wasn't born knowing that it should not jump on the stove or sit in that chair. Deal with these mistakes very gently until you are sure the Siamese trusts you and will be annoyed, but not frightened, when you raise your voice.

To discourage inappropriate behaviors, such as clawing furniture or climbing drapes, introduce the cat or kitten to its climbing and scratching post as soon as possible. Most cats and kittens readily figure out what it's for.

During these first few weeks together you are forming the basis for what can be a true friendship across species lines, a friendship that provides insight into and rewards from a fascinating and loving creature.

THE STAGES OF SIAMESE LIFE

Your Siamese will share your life for some 15 or 20 years. As with people, a cat's needs change as it grows older. Here's what to expect at each stage of your cat's life.

Relation to Human Age

A Siamese goes through the same stages of life as a human—although at a quicker pace—and with many of the same characteristics. The Siamese lifespan is much shorter than that of the human, but a comparison can be made by letting the first year of feline life equal 20 human years and each feline year thereafter, three human years. Thus, a Siamese at three years is roughly the same as a human of 26 years, and Granmaw, a blue point that lived to be 24 years old, was about 90 human years old.

Early Kittenhood

Birth to Three Weeks

Kittenhood lasts from birth to eight months, according to all the cat registries, but growth

Chocolate point is one of four basic colors recognized by some registries in the Siamese breed standard.

and development may continue well beyond that time. During early kittenhood one can see all the stages of human child development. For the first two or three weeks the kittens are focused on the mother, nursing and sleeping and receiving her care. Soon thereafter, they begin to react to her and their siblings, patting her on the nose and making the first awkward attempts at play with each other.

Four to Ten Weeks

The next phase of kittenhood, from about four to ten weeks, finds the kittens gaining in motor skills and becoming very active. They are much like human two- to-three-year-olds, into everything and alternating between periods of frenetic activity and total exhaustion. Toward the end of this phase the most precocious ones in a litter begin to seek human attention; this is the beginning of the socialization phase, which seems to click on somewhere between 12 and 14 weeks. (In reality, their turning to humans for affection is conditioned by handling from birth; without close contact then they would not later become as trusting of humans.)

Late Kittenhood to Puberty

From four to seven months the baby teeth are replaced by the permanent teeth, and by eight months most of the kitten's growth has been attained. Sometime between five and twelve months, puberty usually arrives. Again, the timing is highly variable. Our Stringh Beene, a gentle lilac point that never had an unkind thought, was 18 months old before he had a clue about sex. At the other extreme are the many tales of unexpected litters sired by six-month-old kittens. Whenever puberty happens, it is hard to miss. When the female goes into her first heat cycle (estrus), she calls loudly and rolls on the floor. The male does not have cycles, but when he is sexually mature his urine will take on a much stronger odor, he may start spraying, which is a way of marking territory and advertising for females, and he may become very restless, particularly at night.

Altering

Unless they are to be bred, the young Siamese should be altered soon after puberty. Otherwise, the female will cycle in and out of heat every other week for up to three months, go out for a few months, and then start all over again. The strongest drive in the adult Siamese male is to mate; if he is kept from it, he will be terribly frustrated.

Altering the female, called *spaying*, involves the surgical removal of the female reproductive organs: ovaries, tubes, and uterus. Altering the male, referred to as *neutering*, is castration or removal of the testicles. Veterinarians generally recommend altering female cats at six months and male cats between eight and ten months, although both surgeries can now be performed safely at an earlier age. In fact, some breeders and shelters alter kittens early, before releasing them to new homes, in an effort to prevent indiscriminate breeding.

Aside from helping to curb the pet overpopulation crisis, altering your Siamese can be beneficial in many ways for both sexes. Neutering the male cat:

✔ reduces aggressive and roaming behaviors.

✔ eliminates or decreases certain health risks influenced by breeding and male hormones.

✔ curbs the male's tendency to spray urine as a means of territorial marking.

Spaying the female cat:

✔ eliminates the possibility of unwanted litters of kittens.

✔ eliminates annoying heat cycles.

✔ eliminates or decreases certain health risks influenced by breeding, birthing, and female hormones.

Because they are not obsessed with finding a mate, altered animals typically make better pets and develop deeper attachments to their human caretakers. In addition, their chances of living longer, healthier lives are vastly improved, because they no longer feel the biological urge to roam far and wide in search of a mate. It's a fact that animals allowed to roam freely outside are more likely to get lost, be hit by cars, injured in fights, or exposed to poisons and pathogens.

Young Adulthood to Middle Age

In general, the Siamese is in its physical prime from one to five years. The years from about six to twelve or so can be viewed as middle age, although many Siamese seem not to change at all during this time, except perhaps to put on a little weight. Barring illness, they may remain as playful and active as a four year old.

Advanced Age

The teen years bring the first signs of old age, but not necessarily severe problems. After 12 the Siamese usually slows down a bit, may not look as sleek as it did at five, and should be watched carefully for changes that could indicate disease. At this stage the teeth may start to go, but this is not a serious threat to their health, so long as diseased gums and teeth are treated promptly.

It is not unusual for Siamese to live to be 15 and above. This last stage of Siamese life will see a further gradual decline in activity and an increased concern for the comforts of life—the sunny windowsill should have ample padding for the aging joints and a chair or kitchen step stool nearby to save the effort of jumping that high. If they were fussy about anything before, they will become even fussier in old age, just as we humans do.

Physical Changes

As with people, a cat's rate of metabolism gradually slows with age. The organs typically become less efficient at digesting food or clearing waste products from the body. These physical changes may require some important adjustments to the cat's daily diet to ensure continued good health. Foods labeled *for all life stages* are designed to meet the needs of cats of all ages, from kittens through senior adulthood. But cats, like people, age differently, so there is no single pet food or special *senior* formula that is suitable for all older cats.

Weight

Because energy needs decline with less activity, some middle-aged and senior cats that don't play as much anymore may require fewer calories to avoid becoming obese. There are a number of specialty formula pet foods on the market for weight control and senior care. The higher fiber content in some of these foods is designed to satisfy the cat's appetite so that the animal doesn't feel hungry, even though it is consuming fewer calories, less fat, and generally a little less protein.

Not all cats get fat and need fewer calories as they get older. Some actually grow thinner because their ability to efficiently extract and utilize nutrients in food tends to decline with age. Many older cats have to eat more to get enough energy, because they don't digest their food as well as they used to.

Weight loss may also signal health problems, such as kidney or thyroid disease, both common in older cats. Always have such symptoms investigated promptly by your veterinarian. If your aging cat's condition requires a special diet or treatment plan, your veterinarian can recommend the appropriate course of action.

Euthanasia

It is in this stage in the life of a Siamese that you are most likely to face a very difficult decision: whether to end its life by euthanasia. Your veterinarian can give you information and advice, but the final decision is yours. My best advice is to watch your cat very carefully. When it seems to you that its discomfort is not counterbalanced by some happiness, it is time.

Throughout history, cats have been revered as gods or feared as devils. Both beliefs have been the result of human misunderstanding. To live compatibly with another species, you must first learn its language, and how it perceives its world.

Feline Nature

Cats are neither inscrutable, mysterious, mystical, nor any of those other fanciful designations that would have you think that feline behavior cannot be understood. What rubbish! Of course, cats (even Siamese) can be understood, but in terms of *their* nature, not ours. All it takes is understanding the feline nature, the basics of which are extremely simple and can be understood very quickly. Going beyond the basics can be a mutually satisfying occupation for you and your Siamese and one that will provide many years of delightful discovery, for while the basics are simple, what is built on them can be complex and fascinating.

The Predatory Cat

First of all, cats are predators, which means they are hunters. Even without ever having hunted anything ourselves, we know that

Cats are naturally curious about their environment, a trait that sometimes gets them into trouble.

successful hunting requires keen senses, patience, caution, stealth, quick responses, and the ability to learn.

The Nocturnal Cat

Cats are nocturnal, hunting mostly at night, yet most pet cats adjust to their human's pattern of activity and sleep at night.

Much of the mystery and lore of cats is associated with their mastery of the night. Their unique anatomy gives them superior nighttime hunting prowess, but has also linked them with witchcraft and superstition. A clear understanding of how the cat's primary senses function can put such fears to rest.

Siamese Senses

All five Siamese senses are far superior to ours.

Sight: They have excellent night vision, but cannot see in total darkness. A special layer of cells in the cat's eye called the *tapetum lucidum* reflects all available light and makes the cat able to see well in very dim light. This mirror-light reflector also makes a cat's eyes appear to glow in the dark.

Smell: Blessed with an acute sense of smell, cats also have a special scent organ, called the *Jacobson's organ*, which enables them to taste scent molecules in the air. Located in the roof of the mouth, this organ is believed to help mammals find mates by sniffing out sex hormones called *pheromones*. The snarling grimace a cat displays when sniffing the air with this organ is called the *flehmen* response.

Hearing: Cats can hear frequencies well beyond the range of human hearing. This helps them hone into the whereabouts of small prey. Cats also appear able to recognize and sort out a myriad of sounds in their environment, locating the faint squeak of a sewer rat amidst a cacophony of blaring street noises.

Taste: Experts say that cats can distinguish between salty or sour foods, but sweets are meaningless to them. Tell that to the Siamese that does flips for sugar cookies. Well, it's probably the cookie's fat content that the cat craves, and not the sugar.

Touch: Much more than chin decorations, whiskers are highly sensitive tactile organs, so *never* clip them off your Siamese. Cats use their whiskers to navigate around objects in near darkness and to detect vibrations (as slight as a mouse on the move) in the air around them.

Social Behavior

Cats are social animals. Several studies of groups of cats, both domestic and feral, have shown this, which is quite contrary to the popular idea of the domestic cat as solitary. However, cats can live alone as well as in groups. In cat society there are modes of behavior that serve to minimize fighting and thus the possibility of injury. A major one is the establishment of a dominance-subordinate hierarchy.

While this may involve skirmishes and aggressive behavior in the beginning, in the long run there is less fighting because of the recognition and acceptance of positions in the system.

Communication

Communication among members is essential to any society, including feline. Cats communicate with each other through body position, movement, and scent; through facial expression; and by voice. Any one or combinations of these can inform others of a range of intention from challenge to proposal of friendship or more.

Territoriality

Then there is territoriality, an aspect of feline nature that relates to predation and communication. Studies of wild cats show that they have home ranges, which is common among predatory species. As they move about their range, cats leave scent marks along the way. These may be urine containing a special oily substance, which is sprayed onto upright objects from a standing position, or scent from skin glands on the head, tail, and paws, which is transferred to objects as the cat rubs or scratches them. These chemical messages are "read" by others through the vomeronasal gland, which is a small sac of olfactory tissue with openings just behind the upper incisors. In order to get the scent molecules into the gland, the cat lifts its upper lip, opens its mouth slightly, and sniffs; this is called the *flehmen* response.

Mothering

Finally, there is the behavior of mothers toward their kittens. The purring, kneading, and "presenting" (turning the rear toward another) of adults can be traced to the instinctive behavior of young kittens and mothers. There is evidence that the sound of purring by the kittens promotes the release of milk from the mother's glands, as does the repeated pressing with their hands as they nurse. At this stage, the queen grooms the kittens frequently, particularly the perianal region, which results in the evacuation of the urinary bladder and the bowel. The kitten learns that these activities lead to satisfaction and relief, and they become part of its body language as an adult.

Behavior Analysis

Let us apply this basic information to the behavior of Simon, the typical young, altered Siamese in typical home situations.

✔ Olivia, Simon's person, comes home every workday at six. Simon is always waiting at the door to greet her (*keen hearing*) and rubs against her ankles (*marking and claiming as part of his territory*). He usually talks to her in high-pitched, strident tones (*Hi, Mom. I'm glad you're home. Feed me, feed me, feed me!*).

✔ Olivia understands what Simon is saying and also knows that he has accepted her as a surrogate cat-mother. Being a good Siamese person, she immediately opens a can of Simon's favorite food and puts down a dish of it, giving him a little extra because he's obviously so hungry. Simon wolfs it down (*eat as much as you can as fast as you can before somebody bigger and fiercer comes along*), but fills up before he can finish the last bit. He stands over the dish and makes swiping motions on the floor toward

it (*gotta cover up these leftovers before the smell attracts somebody bigger or fiercer*).

✔ Finally satisfied that he has swiped around the dish enough, he saunters into the living room to his favorite chair, going not directly across but around the sides of the room (*there's danger in open spaces; keep to cover whenever possible*).

✔ After a nap and helping Olivia watch TV, Simon visits his litter box. When he is done, he covers up the soiled litter (*can't give those predators a clue that you're in the neighborhood*).

✔ To a Siamese, cleanliness is way beyond godliness. Some have been known to refuse to enter a dirty box, leaving their deposits on the floor beside the box (*dirty feet, smelly trail, and the next thing you know T. Rex is on top of you!*). In fact, cats can be trained to use the people toilet, particularly if they try to perch on the edge of even a clean litter box, which indicates they do not like the litter under their feet.

✔ Olivia feels sorry for Simon, home by himself all day (*cats sleep about 18 hours a day*), and decides to get him a buddy. She calls his breeder and, sure enough, there is a little

Total body language: Top, left to right: At ease, friendly mood. Uncertain, slightly apprehensive. Bottom, left to right: Apprehensive. Threatened, frightened.

Siamese are natural climbers but should be kept safely indoors. The indoor cat needs a substitute to climb on, such as a carpeted cat climbing tree.

Cat's pupils open wide to let in all available light for nighttime hunting.

Siamese cats are very vocal by nature and possess a repertoire of distinct sounds.

It is usually easier to introduce a kitten into a household where an adult cat already resides. The adult may even teach the kitten a thing or two.

Having two cats allows you to observe the way they communicate and interact with each other.

Feline etiquette. Top: Asking permission with licks. Bottom: Showing disrespect.

brother ready for a new home. Olivia is so pleased to present him to Simon. Simon, however, is something less than pleased by this surprise (*surprises can mean danger*), hisses, runs away, and hides (*I never smelled him before, how do I know what he might do to me?*).

✔ The new kitten, now named Legree, and Simon gradually make friends as Simon discovers that Legree is really just a little cat and not some small but vicious predator. Soon, Simon is grooming Legree (*social behavior*) and playing with him (*teaching him to hunt and fight*).

Eventually, they will become buddies. One, not necessarily the older, will become the dominant one, but very likely they will share dominance, one being top cat in certain places or situations and being subordinate in others. Our Poopsie, Tai Phoon Ta-nuk, our founding queen, was the perfect example. In her middle age she became low cat in the house, but when Poopsie boarded the boat, our summer home, she was immediately, and without dispute, top cat.

Acquired Behavior

Despite all the biological imperatives, the overriding characteristic of the Siamese is its ability to learn. It can learn to trust a human as much as its mother. If its person fosters that trust and affection, the Siamese will become a constant, delightful companion and a source of pleasure all its life and beyond.

The Language of Cats

Knowing some of the language of cats is much more fun than learning a foreign human language. Cat-watching takes on an added dimension. Your Siamese were already pleasing to the eye and the hand, but now you can understand what they are communicating to each other. Better yet, on occasion you can join in the conversation.

Body Language

Much of cat language is expressed by the body.

✔ A stiff-legged stance with head and tail extended, staring eyes with contracted pupils, and ears up and turned back is a serious challenge.

✔ If the cat's tail bushes and the hair along the spine rises up, stand clear, as it is on the verge of attacking. A cat so enraged has no access to its reason, will not recognize a beloved human or cat buddy, and will attack even a fleeing, submissive cat. Indoors this rarely happens, but the rage center in the brain can be set off by the scent from one male to another and by the threat of one cat to another's young kitten.

✔ At the other end of this confrontation range is extreme submissiveness. The ears are flattened out to the sides, the pupils are dilated, and the cat crouches or rolls over, perhaps to protect itself from the feared attack. This is not the time to try to join in the conversation. Do not try to touch them, but put a dustmop, a coat, or a heavy throw rug between them to break the spell of rage and fear and to separate them.

Friendly language: Body language that sends friendly messages is much more common and certainly more welcome. The friendly face has an open look, the size of the pupils is appropriate to the light level, and the ears are erect and forward. The body is relaxed or the back slightly arched, with the tail up like a flagpole. The ultimate in friendliness is the slow blink. While looking into your eyes, the cat will slowly close and then open its eyes. We don't have tails to signal with, but we can certainly return the slow blink or even initiate a friendly exchange. Even fearful strays will respond if you crouch down (to appear less threatening) and give them repeated slow blinks.

Grooming

Mutual grooming is another expression of friendliness, and one in which humans, armed with a brush or comb, can join, although being washed by the rough tongue of a Siamese can be hard to take, however flattering.

Rules of Etiquette

Cats have etiquette, also. When one cat is in place and a second wants to join it, the polite behavior is for the second cat to approach, give the settled cat two or three licks on the head or neck, and wait in the standing position. If the response is a return of the licks, that means, "You are welcome to join me." If the response is just calmness, that means, "Okay, but don't crowd me." A mean look, low

growl, or more overt displeasure obviously means, "Permission denied."

When cats approach each other, the polite thing to do is touch noses. If they are good friends, they may rub heads and necks. On the other hand, a full stare is an insult. But the biggest insult of all is when one cat sticks its nose right into the body fur of another and then does the *flehmen* response.

Vocal Language

Studies of cat vocalizations describe 16 different voice patterns. (There may be more distinguishable by cats.) These are classified as murmur patterns, vowel patterns, and strained-intensity sounds.

Murmurs: The murmurs include purring and other closed-mouth sounds associated with contentment and friendliness. A queen talking to her kittens uses many of these.

Vowel sounds: The vowel sounds account for most of the conversational vocalizing of the cat, for which the Siamese is justly famous. A multitude of cat words such as *meeow, yow, mow, ngow,* and *mow-wow,* indicate greetings, requests, demands, denials, and frustration.

Strained intensity sounds: The strained-intensity sounds are those used in attack and defense—hisses, growls, and screams—and in mating. The call of a female in heat can sound like a bugle and travel just about as far. The male calls also, and when a female in heat is within range, sings a high-pitched, chirrupy love song. The scream-roar of the female as copulation is completed is unique. Quite different, but also unique, is the chatter, usually elicited by seeing a bird or a squirrel. Dear Phusatti was a great huntress of flies and always chattered and clacked before bringing down her prey.

NUTRITION

With cats, as with all living things, good health requires good nutrition. This means not only the right nutrients, but the right proportions of nutrients to each other, and the proper total amount of them.

Feline Nutrients

Nutrients, which are substances that provide nourishment, include proteins and amino acids, carbohydrates, lipids (fats), vitamins, minerals, and even water. These categories are the same both for humans and for other mammals, such as dogs. Because of this, people sometimes think that a cat can be fed a diet of table scraps or dog food. This is wrong! Cats have a metabolism that is quite different in many ways from that of dogs and humans and consequently have dietary requirements that are distinctly feline. The most famous (or infamous) case involved a young cat that was going blind; the veterinarian discovered that its owners were vegetarians and were feeding the cat a vegetarian diet. Happily, further research led to the discovery of the requirement of the amino acid taurine for the maintenance of vision as well as heart function. As the name taurine (Taurus, the bull) indicates, this is not an amino acid that occurs in soybeans and lettuce.

Cats are carnivores, not vegetarians. They must have meat to maintain good health.

Another important difference between cats and dogs is the cat's much higher requirement for lipids. Some studies indicate that a kitten needs a diet that is 30 percent or more lipid. Not only do they need more fat than other species, but they must have some animal fat in the diet. Again, plant oils are lipids, but they are different from those produced in animals. A carnivore's metabolism requires animal nutrients. If this presents a problem for strict vegetarians, they should get a pet that is a natural vegetarian, not a cat.

Commercial Foods

While feline nutrition is an entire field of study on its own, we do not have to be experts to provide the proper diet for our Siamese. Commercial cat foods today are researched and formulated to provide enough animal protein and other essential nutrients needed for good feline health. The Association of American Feed Control Officials (AAFCO) has established cat food nutrient profiles, testing protocols, and labeling regulations for the pet food industry to follow. The major pet food manufacturers use AAFCO's nutrient profiles and testing protocols

TIP

Feline Nutritional Needs

Cats are carnivores; they must have animal protein and animal amino acids.

as the standard for formulating and substantiating the nutrient content of their products.

The pet food industry offers many well-formulated commercial cat foods that are 100 percent nutritionally complete and balanced for cats. These come in three basic types:

✔ canned (wet)
✔ semimoist (also called soft-dry)
✔ dry.

Aside from these three basic types, cat foods are also packaged and marketed according to whether they are generic (economy brands), popular (supermarket brands), or premium brands. The premium brands, sold primarily through pet stores and veterinarians, are generally considered to contain higher-quality ingredients, but they are the most expensive.

The nutrient contents of many commercial cat foods are also formulated to meet specific life-cycle needs of cats, from kittens through old age. Growth and reproduction formulas satisfy the higher protein needs of growing kittens and pregnant or nursing queens. Foods labeled for *all life stages of cats* meet these requirements because they encompass the full range of nutritional needs for cats of all ages. However, foods labeled for adult *maintenance* are not satisfactory fare for kittens or pregnant cats, because they contain a lower protein content. These foods, usually marketed for weight control,

mature cats, or senior care, are intended primarily for full-grown, nonbreeding, less active, overweight, or older felines. Other specialty formulas, such as those for hairball control, dental care, and urinary tract health, must still state on the label whether the food is intended for all life stages of cats or for adult maintenance.

Dry Versus Wet Foods

Several years ago, dry foods were linked with urinary tract problems because of their "high ash content." The ash content of anything is what is left after incineration—the minerals. Obviously, cats must have calcium, phosphorus, potassium, magnesium, and other elements, which provide structural support and cellular function. But since urinary gravel, which can cause bleeding and blockage of the urinary tract (Feline Urologic Syndrome, FUS) and death of the cat, is made of minerals, it was logical to suspect that minerals were at fault. Research in this area was very successful in finding that magnesium was the culprit. Cat-food manufacturers modified their formulations to lower magnesium content in both wet and dry foods. (Magnesium in small quantities is essential to life, so it cannot be eliminated altogether.) The amount of magnesium is listed on the labels of all the good-quality foods. The general rule is that magnesium should be less than 0.1 percent of the diet or no more than 230 mg/1000 Kcal. As long as this requirement is met, it does not matter whether the food is wet or dry. Of course, a cat eating dry food will need more water, as canned foods are about 78 percent water.

Another consideration when choosing between wet and dry foods is convenience. Because of the very low water content of dry food, bacteria cannot grow in it, and it can be left without spoiling. There is some evidence that eating dry food helps keep the teeth clean.

Finally, there is the cat's preference. My Charlie refuses to eat canned food. If I put some down for him, he takes one sniff and proceeds to try to cover it up, swiping the floor all around the dish. The message is very clear. His grandmother, Phussati, also preferred dry food, but lost most of her teeth when she was in her teens. A little water added to her plate of crunchies turned them into mushies, and the problem was solved.

Semimoist Foods

Semimoist foods come in soft-dry nuggets packaged in foil-lined wrappers or bags. These products attempt to combine the convenience and palatability of the dry and canned types, making them an attractive, middle-of-the-road choice for the human consumer to use. They contain more moisture than dry foods, but not enough to cause the odors and spoilage associated with canned foods.

Dyes

One last word about dry food: Avoid those that have coloring added. My Siamese get upset stomachs from the dyes that are added to some dry foods. These dyes are not nutrients; they are put there to please the eye of the purchaser. Choose instead the unappealing (to our eye), uncolored, drab foods that, at least, will not leave permanent orange stains on carpet or upholstery if a starving Siamese eats too much too fast and "upchucks."

Siamese prefer a regular place for their food and water.

======== TIP ========

Propylene Glycol

When first introduced to the market, semimoist foods contained *propylene glycol*, a preservative used in cosmetics and alcoholic beverages. This substance acted primarily as a humectant, preserving the moisture retention in the soft-dry foods. But when the chemical was implicated in causing red blood cell damage in cats, its use in cat foods was discontinued. Today, other preservatives are used in these foods to prevent mold and bacterial growth and improve shelf life.

Some breeders feed only dry food and others both dry and wet. If you feel confused or uncertain about what to feed, ask your veterinarian and the breeder of your Siamese for recommendations and advice.

Cat Food Label Basics

Pet food companies are required by law to supply certain nutritional information on their labels to help consumers make informed choices. For example, the label must disclose

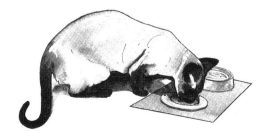

To avoid fighting, every cat in the household should have its own food dish.

Adult indoor cats usually do well on an adult maintenance commercial cat food, which has less protein and calories than the growth formulas for kittens.

whether the food is formulated to provide *complete and balanced* nutrition. The word *complete* means the food has all the necessary nutrients a cat needs for good health. The word *balanced* means those necessary nutrients are present in the proper proportions. Look for these words on any cat food you buy. If the label doesn't say the food is *complete and balanced*, assume that it isn't.

To prove that their products provide *complete and balanced nutrition*, pet food manufacturers must either adhere to a proven pet food formula or test-feed their products to live cats for a specified period of time. The nutritional adequacy statement discloses which method was used, saying something similar to: *Animal feeding tests using Association of American Feed Control Officials' procedures substantiate that [this food] provides complete and balanced nutrition for all life stages of cats.*

Ingredients

Ingredients are supposed to be listed on the label in descending order of predominance by weight; however, this can be somewhat misleading. For example, meat may be listed first, leading the consumer to believe the product contains mostly meat, when in reality, the summation of separately listed grains and cereals makes plant material the predominant ingredient. Also, some labeling terms are strictly regulated, while others are not.

Amount and Frequency of Feeding

Once you find good foods that your Siamese likes, the only remaining problem is to resist

For the first full year of its life, a kitten needs to be fed a high quality, high protein cat food formulated specifically for feline growth and reproduction.

If you want your Siamese to stay off of kitchen countertops, use a sharp-sounding "No!" Be firm and consistent in your training, but never, never hit your cat.

White toes or spots are considered a flaw in the Siamese breed standard and can't be shown as such. However, a separate breed called the Snowshoe features both the pointed pattern and white paws.

CHECKLIST

Schedules

1 A twice-a-day feeding schedule is usual for adults, although some feed only once and others three times. A bowl of fresh water should be available at all times.

2 Kittens and young cats up to the time when full growth is attained need to be fed more freely and more frequently. At this stage it is better to err on the side of excess food than not enough.

3 Females in the second half of pregnancy and lactating females should have as much food as they want, as should all cats that are recuperating from surgery or an illness.

4 As your cat ages, it becomes less active and needs fewer calories to maintain its optimum weight. There are several commercial cat foods that are formulated with fewer calories for the less active cat.

5 The watchword is vigilance. The owner must be mindful of the cat's condition and adjust its diet to suit its changing needs.

overfeeding it. Some Siamese have a normal governor on their appetites, but others eat as though starvation is just around the corner. Your veterinarian can measure the height of your cat and give you its optimum weight. In general, Siamese females in good shape are 5 to 7 pounds (2.3–3.2 kg), and the males, 8 to 10 pounds (3.6–4.5 kg), depending on the size of their bone structure.

TIP

Dietary Changes

✔ To start any dietary change, mix small amounts of the new food with your cat's current rations.

✔ Gradually, over a period of a week or two, increase the amount of new food as you decrease the amount of old food until the changeover is complete.

Guide to Feeding

The best guide to how much to feed your cat is the cat's appearance. The Siamese in good trim should have a tubular body, not a fat or saggy one. It should not be so thin that there are hollows in front of its hips. When you run the palm of your hand down its back, you should not feel individual vertebrae. Once your Siamese is in good shape, note its weight for future reference. (Your veterinarian has small animal scales, or you can stand on your own bathroom scales while holding the cat, note the combined weight, then release the cat and subtract your weight.)

Make Dietary Changes Gradually

With so many life cycle choices, product lines, flavors, and varieties to choose from, the important thing to remember is that no one perfect pet food exists for every cat and for every owner. Cats have individual needs, as do humans, and those needs are likely to change over time. During every routine health checkup, review your cat's diet with your veterinarian and have him or her reevaluate whether any changes are needed.

If your veterinarian recommends changing your cat's diet, do so gradually, over a period of at least a week or more. Sudden changes in diet or feeding routine may cause some animals to experience gastrointestinal upset or other distress. Or, your Siamese may simply turn up its nose at the new food and refuse to eat it.

A Warning About Obesity

Obesity is considered the number one nutritional disorder among companion animals today in the United States. As in humans, the extra pounds put pets at higher risk for certain health conditions, such as diabetes, heart disease, lameness, and joint problems, among other ills. Obesity can also increase the risks of anesthesia and surgical complications, should your cat need an operation. The added health risks may even contribute to a shorter lifespan in your Siamese. That's why it's important to acknowledge when your Siamese is growing too heavy and make the necessary dietary adjustments, based on your veterinarian's advice.

Too Fat?

In general, a cat is too fat if you cannot feel its ribs without having to probe with your fingers through thick, fleshy layers. Fat cats also often have sagging, pendulous bellies, bulges around the neck, and heavy accumulations of fat at the base of the tail. Your veterinarian can best judge your Siamese's overall body condition, so ask for a frank assessment at

═══ TIP ═══

Indoor Cats and Obesity

Indoor cats have fewer opportunities for natural exercise, such as climbing trees, so it's important to provide substitute playgrounds for them in your home. The best ones are those fancy, carpeted cat trees or "kitty condos," special furniture built for cats that serves as jungle gym, scratching post, and sleeping quarters. The well-built, sturdy versions are expensive, but usually well worth the investment.

each checkup. A physical exam is important because certain underlying medical conditions can sometimes contribute to weight problems. For example, *hypothyroidism*, caused by an underactive thyroid gland, slows down the body's metabolism, causing weight gain and sluggishness.

Basically, cats get fat for the same reasons people do: too much food and too little exercise. Some cats, especially those deprived of food as kittens, do not have an off switch for their appetites. They will overeat if you leave out too much dry food for them to consume free-choice, so you have to be vigilant about controlling their portions. For such cats, measure and leave out only the recommended daily ration. Use the feeding guidelines on the product's packaging as a general guide to portion size, keeping in mind that you may have to adjust the amounts based on your cat's individual needs.

The outdoor environment is so filled with hazards that no Siamese should ever be allowed outside without supervision. The thought of speeding traffic, wild predators, malicious people, dogs, poisons, disease, and parasites should be enough to prompt any Siamese owner to keep it indoors.

Ingestible Hazards

The indoor environment, while infinitely safer, still may harbor hazards for the Siamese. Chief among these are things that can be ingested. Siamese are noted for a healthy appetite and superabundant curiosity. This means that many things other than food get put into their little mouths. These ingestible dangers may be categorized as mechanical or chemical.

Mechanical Hazards

Mechanical hazards include small objects that could choke the cat or those that could pierce or block the digestive tract. These include toys that have small metal or plastic parts that can be detached and loose buttons and coins. Loose bits of yarn, string, or twine can cause obstruction or strangulation of the bowel. Do not leave a sewing basket or pin cushion around the house. Not only is yarn, string, or thread fun

The seal point sports striking dark-colored extremities against a lighter body color.

(and dangerous) to play with, but pins and needles are also attractive, especially needles that are threaded. The cat begins by biting the thread, which gets tangled on its rough tongue, and ends up swallowing thread and needle, often resulting in deadly consequences.

Bones: Small bones can choke, pierce the digestive tract, and cause blockage. Poultry bones are notorious for splintering as they break; the sharp, pointed ends can be driven through the wall of the intestine by its contractions or lodge crosswise and obstruct the bowel. Either case is obviously life-threatening.

Chemical Hazards

The ingestible chemical hazards are poisons. The problem here is not so much the widely known poisons, such as lye and antifreeze, but the ones we accept as nonhazardous that are poisonous to cats.

Phenol: Some popular household cleaners contain phenol. This compound and its relatives (look for the word *phenol* within longer chemical compound names) are not only toxic to cats but accumulate in their tissues over time. Eventually a level will be reached that causes damage to her liver, kidneys, and other organs. Read the labels of your cleaning solutions and household disinfectants.

Medications: Do not be tempted to give any human or canine medication to a cat, unless it is prescribed by your veterinarian. Our common headache and fever remedies, aspirin and acetaminophen, are poisonous to cats. Feline metabolism is very different from ours and other omnivores; they lack the enzymes that other species have that break down certain compounds before they can reach a toxic level.

Poisons: A complete list of poisons would go on for pages and probably be skipped over by many readers. Instead, consider the following as guidelines (with a few examples) to identifying household poisons:

✔ Anything with a label that includes "Keep out of the reach of children"

✔ Anything that is intended to kill other organisms (insecticides, fungicides, pesticides, herbicides, mothballs, rat poison, slug bait)

✔ Lawn chemicals, such as weed killers and fertilizers can poison pets that walk in treated areas, then lick the chemicals off their paws. Read lawn care and pesticide product labels carefully before using. Avoid letting your Siamese outdoors to pad through freshly treated areas until the first rain or the next thorough watering has rinsed the substance away.

✔ Preservatives and disinfectants (wood preservative, formaldehyde, phenol)

✔ Strong acids (muriatic, battery) and strong alkalis (drain cleaners, oven cleaners, permanent-wave solution, paint remover)

✔ Strong oxidants (undiluted bleach, peroxide)

✔ Organic (fat-dissolving) solvents (dry-cleaning fluids, gasoline, home-heating oil, kerosene, turpentine, nail-polish remover, paint thinners)

✔ Paints and polishes

✔ Alcohols, particularly methanol and ethylene glycol (antifreeze, rubbing alcohol, windshield-washer fluid)

Antifreeze

No discussion about chemical hazards to animals would be complete without antifreeze. Ethylene glycol, the prime ingredient in traditional antifreeze, is very poisonous to animals. To make matters worse, the substance tastes sweet, so it attracts animals to drink. This means that if your car has even a tiny cooling system leak, you may put your own cat (if you allow it to go outdoors), or your neighbors' pets, at grave risk. To avoid this, immediately hose down or wipe up all fluid leaks and antifreeze spills, no matter how small. When adding fluids to your car, use a funnel to prevent spills.

Safer brands: Consider replacing your car's traditional antifreeze with a safer antifreeze brand. Safer antifreeze products on the market contain *propylene glycol*, which is significantly less toxic than ethylene glycol.

Note: The possibility of accidental antifreeze poisoning is just one more reason why you should keep your Siamese safely indoors. Even if your own Siamese is strictly an indoor cat, using a safer antifreeze product in your car is a humane practice that will benefit other free-roaming domestic animals and wildlife.

Poisonous Plants

Other ingestible chemical hazards are more subtly and enticingly packaged in certain plants, including a number of popular house-plants. Among these poisonous plants are

- azaleas
- caladiums
- common or cherry laurel
- dumb cane (Dieffenbachia)
- ivies
- mistletoe
- oleander
- philodendrons
- rhododendrons.

Poinsettia has long been thought to be poisonous, but recent evidence indicates it may be an irritant with low toxicity. However, when in doubt, avoid risk. Since no cat can resist at least biting a dangling leaf at eye level (and eye level to a Siamese is anywhere it can get to), the safest plan is to banish all poisonous houseplants, cut flowers, and greenery, even dried, from your home. If this is not acceptable, put the plants in a separate room or hang them out of Siamese reach. For a list of poisonous plants, check the Animal Poison Control Center at *www.aspca.org.*

Other Hazards

Electrical: Electrical cords are a serious hazard if the Siamese tries to chew on them. They are especially attractive to kittens. Hide all cords, or put them out of reach. If your Siamese is a wire chewer, unplug the cords in the room in which it is left alone. Less common, but just as serious, is the electrical outlet or receptacle. Spraying males have been known to use an open receptacle as a target, resulting in a severe burn to the genitals, not to mention damage to the receptacle and the danger of an electrical fire. Open receptacles should be

closed with the small caps designed to protect children from electrical shock.

Drowning: There is not much danger of an adult Siamese drowning indoors, unless you have an indoor pool or are careless about what is in the washing machine when you start it up, but kittens have been known to drown in toilet bowls and sump pumps. So, if you have a young Siamese, keep the lid down and do not leave filled bathtubs unattended. Make sure sump pumps are securely covered, too.

Miscellaneous: There are many miscellaneous hazards in any household. Open fireplaces, even cold, are dangerous, as cats may be tempted to explore the chimney. Household appliances of all sorts can be hazards. I never close the refrigerator door without checking for Siamese tails in the way. Beware of the possibility of closing your cat in a washing machine, dishwasher, clothes dryer, or cold oven. Hot stoves and ovens, space heaters, any open flame, and electric fans are obvious dangers.

Collars: Cat collars are my final hazard item. Flea collars have been known to cause skin irritation and loss of hair. I see no reason for an indoor cat to have any kind of collar, but if you must put one on your Siamese, be certain that it is properly adjusted, preferably the type that will break away under the weight of the cat if snagged, and has no bell. Wearing a bell has been linked to stomach ulcers in cats, and too-loose collars can cause death by hanging or choking if the collar snags on some projection. I have read of cats dying from getting their lower jaw caught under a collar. The collar should be adjusted so that you can fit just one finger under it without causing the cat discomfort, but no looser.

HEALTH CARE

Your Siamese will need regular vaccinations and health checkups from your veterinarian. Proper preventive care is essential for your cat's physical and emotional well-being. You also need to learn about the diseases that affect cats.

Preventive Health Care

Three simple preventive health care strategies can help maximize the chances of your Siamese living a longer and healthier life:

1. Keep your Siamese indoors.

2. Get annual veterinary checkups for your Siamese.

3. Adhere to the routine vaccination schedule your veterinarian recommends.

The first strategy is common sense. An indoor cat is less likely to contract an illness from a free-roaming animal or fall victim to the many hazards inherent in the great outdoors. But keeping your Siamese indoors doesn't mean you can skip routine veterinary checkups and regular vaccinations. They are just as important for the indoor cat because some disease organisms are airborne, or they can be carried in on your hands or clothing.

Some Siamese fans prefer cats with a rounder look, rather than the slender, wedge-headed types seen in show halls.

Vaccinations

These days, veterinarians tailor vaccination requirements to each individual cat's needs, based on factors such as the cat's age, health status, and risk of exposure. For example, a cat's risk of exposure is higher if it is used for breeding, travels to cat shows, is allowed outdoors, or lives with other cats. Also, instead of annual booster shots, some vaccinations are now being administered every three years, depending on the product used. Your veterinarian can recommend a booster schedule that is best for your Siamese.

Vaccines were first made from viruses, but now include preparations of parts of viral coats, attenuated or killed bacteria, and other pathogenic microorganisms. When a vaccine is put into a cat, it challenges the cat's immune system, which then multiplies the white blood cells that can neutralize the pathogen represented by the vaccine. Some of these cells are maintained on reserve, so to speak, for months and are called memory cells. Should the cat be exposed to that pathogen, the memory cells are ready to mount an attack against the invaders. To keep up an effective level of memory cells, yearly revaccinations (boosters) are needed in most cases.

The American Association of Feline Practitioners and the Academy of Feline Medicine Advisory Panel on Feline Vaccinations highly recommend vaccinating *all* cats for rabies, feline distemper, feline herpes virus (rhinotracheitis), and feline calcivirus. Protection against the latter three is usually administered in a three-in-one vaccine, so that the cat need endure only the one needle stick. Vaccines available for protection against certain other diseases may be considered on an individual basis if, for example, the cat has a heightened risk of becoming infected.

Establishing Immunity

Newborn kittens are born with what is called *passive immunity*, which they acquire from maternal antibodies in their mother's first milk, the *colostrum.* How long this naturally acquired passive immunity lasts depends upon the antibody level in the mother's blood when the kittens are born. Usually, this protection lasts from 12 to 16 weeks, but it may wear off as early as six or eight weeks.

Because kittens are highly susceptible to certain infectious diseases, veterinarians typically recommend giving initial vaccinations at around six to eight weeks of age, to ensure that youngsters remain protected. However, if maternal antibodies are still present in the kitten's system when it receives its first shots, those passive antibodies may render the vaccines ineffective. That's why vaccinations for the common feline respiratory infections and feline distemper are repeated at about 12 weeks of age, to ensure that they *take*, as well as to provide the kitten with continuous immunity as maternal antibodies wear off.

Your Siamese kitten should already have at least one round of the three-in-one vaccines for feline distemper, feline herpes virus, and calcivirus before the breeder lets you bring it home. Ask for a copy of the vaccination records, and be sure to follow up with your own veterinarian for all remaining shots and boosters, as recommended.

Serious Feline Diseases

Following is a brief overview of some major feline diseases for which vaccines are available.

Rabies: One of few feline ailments transmissible to humans, rabies occurs in nearly all warm-blooded animals. Skunks, foxes, raccoons, cats, and dogs account for most sporadic outbreaks in the United States, and most states have laws requiring vaccination for pets to prevent the disease. After the initial vaccination, boosters may be given annually or every three years, depending on local laws and on the vaccine product used.

In an infected animal, the deadly rabies virus travels to the brain, where the disease takes characteristic forms: furious and paralytic, or *dumb*, rabies. In the furious form, cats exhibit personality changes that progress from subtle to severe. While symptoms can vary, normally affectionate and sociable cats may withdraw and hide. Aloof cats may become more loving, but in a few days, most infected animals become irritable and dangerously aggressive. They often act frenzied and deranged and will attack viciously without provocation. With the dumb form, paralysis overtakes the body, starting with the face, jaw, and throat muscles. Unable to swallow its own saliva, the afflicted feline may *foam at the mouth* or, more typically, drool saliva that looks like strings of egg white. Eventually, the rear legs give way, and the cat can no longer stand or walk. Death soon follows.

The rabies virus is transmitted in an infected animal's saliva through a bite, open wound, or scrape. People bitten or scratched by a rabid animal must immediately undergo a series of injections in order to save their lives, for beyond a certain stage, the disease is inevitably fatal. Whenever a human life is at stake, an animal suspected of having rabies is humanely destroyed, and its brain tissue is tested to confirm the presence of the virus.

Some state laws allow the confiscation of any cat that is reported to have scratched or bitten someone. Animals that have been vaccinated for the disease may be quarantined and observed for a period of time. But if the owner cannot furnish proof that the animal was vaccinated, the cat may be destroyed and tested. This should be reason enough to vaccinate any Siamese, even strictly indoor cats, although their risk of contracting the disease is minimal. If you allow your Siamese to go outdoors, it should certainly be immunized against rabies.

Feline distemper: Also called *feline panleukopenia virus (FPV)* or *feline parvovirus*, this illness bears no relation to the virus that causes distemper in dogs. The disease is destructive, highly contagious, and often fatal. Fortunately, it is less common than it once was, thanks, no doubt, to effective and more widespread vaccination.

Early signs of infection may include appetite loss, depression, fever, and vomiting yellow

TIP

Assessing Your Cat's Health Risks

Any change in your cat's lifestyle, such as the addition of a new cat to your household, may require adjustments in your vaccination and booster program. To accurately assess your cat's health risks, your veterinarian needs to know

✔ how often your Siamese is allowed outdoors, if ever
✔ how often your Siamese travels with you
✔ how often your Siamese is exposed to other cats through window screens, cat shows, boarding kennels, or elsewhere
✔ if you plan to use your Siamese for breeding

By knowing the individual details about how your Siamese lives, your veterinarian can recommend the most appropriate vaccination plan.

bile. Because the virus often attacks the lining of the small intestine, the disease also is sometimes referred to as *feline infectious enteritis*. An afflicted cat will show signs of having a painful abdomen and may cry out pitifully if touched in that area. A lowered white blood cell count (leukopenia) confirms the diagnosis and gives the disease its clinical name.

Feline herpesvirus: Also known as *feline viral rhinotracheitis*, this serious upper respiratory infection caused by a herpes virus is characterized by sneezing, nasal discharge, and crusty, watering eyes. Often, the cat stops eating. Highly contagious, this disease spreads

Vaccinations are important health safeguards, and help prevent serious, potentially life-threatening diseases.

easily from cat to cat through direct contact with body secretions and contaminated objects, such as litter boxes, feeding bowls, or even

human hands. It has a high mortality rate among kittens and older cats, which is why vaccination is so important. Cats that survive the acute illness may become chronic carriers and, during stressful periods, will shed the herpes virus, making them a potential hazard to other cats in the household.

Feline calcivirus: Like rhinotracheitis, feline calcivirus is a serious upper respiratory infection with similar symptoms, except it is more likely to progress to pneumonia. Painful tongue and mouth ulcers can make the disease particularly disabling, as the cat may refuse to eat or drink. Muscle soreness, exhibited by a stiff gait or limping, also may be present. Some cats that

Keeping your Siamese on a regular vaccination schedule is important, especially when you have more than one cat.

A lovely lynx point with the characteristic tabby striping.

recover from a calcivirus infection may become carriers. The best prevention is vaccination.

Chlamydia: Sometimes called *feline pneumonitis*, this respiratory infection often begins with weepy eyes and swollen eyelids. The disease can be quite contagious, especially among kittens; however, only a small percentage of feline respiratory infections in the United States are actually caused by chlamydia. The vaccine is considered optional and may be administered based on the cat's risk of exposure.

Feline leukemia virus (FeLV): First discovered in 1964, FeLV suppresses the bone marrow and the immune system, rendering its victims vulnerable to various cancers, such as leukemia, and other secondary ailments. There is no cure. The disease passes from cat to cat through bite wounds and prolonged casual contact. Symptoms vary but generally include weight loss, anemia, poor appetite, lethargy, and recurring infections. An infected cat may seem healthy for years before finally succumbing to a FeLV-related illness.

Testing is available to determine FeLV status with reasonable accuracy, although an occasional false positive or false negative result is possible. To help prevent the spread of the disease, all cats should be tested to ensure their negative status before being introduced into a new household with other felines. Kittens should be tested and certified free of the disease prior to purchase or adoption, as they can acquire the virus from an infected mother. Cats that test positive for FeLV should either be euthanized or kept indoors and isolated from FeLV-negative cats, even vaccinated ones. The disease is not spread from cats to people.

The first FeLV vaccine took about 20 years to develop. Initial immunity is usually established with two injections spaced about a month apart, then maintained by regular boosters. Cats allowed outdoors have the highest risk of exposure and certainly should be vaccinated. Others at risk include those living in multicat households and those exposed to outdoor cats, whether through direct contact or through screened windows. To be safe, any cat that comes into contact with other cats at cat shows or boarding kennels, or through breeding programs, needs protection. Breeding toms and queens should be tested and certified free of the virus.

TIP

FeLV Vaccine

While the rabies vaccine is required by law in many localities, the FeLV is optional. Only you, the owner, can decide whether to vaccinate your Siamese for the leukemia virus. Discuss the pros and cons with your veterinarian, and as you consider the option, keep in mind that FeLV is high on the list of killer diseases in cats. If your Siamese gets the disease, there is no cure.

Feline infectious peritonitis (FIP): This potentially fatal illness strikes primarily younger and older cats and those debilitated by other illnesses, such as feline leukemia virus. Common signs include fever, lethargy, appetite and weight loss, and an overall unhealthy appearance. The disease typically takes one of two forms, wet or dry. The wet form involves fluid buildup in the abdomen and chest. An afflicted cat exhibits labored breathing, extreme depression, and a swollen belly. The dry form progresses more slowly and affects many organs, including the liver, kidneys, pancreas, brain, and eyes. Because symptoms are often vague, the dry form is more difficult to diagnose. The first FIP vaccine became available in 1991 and is given in nasal drops. It is not given as a routine vaccination unless the exposure threat is high. The disease poses a greater hazard in catteries and multicat households, so if this applies to you, discuss this vaccine option with your veterinarian.

Feline immunodeficiency virus (FIV): Also called *feline AIDS*, FIV infects only cats and is *not* transmissible to people. Among cats, the disease appears to be transmitted mainly through bites. Because they engage in mating rituals and territorial fighting, free-roaming intact males have the highest risk of contracting FIV. Cats kept indoors have a low risk of becoming infected, which is another sound reason to keep your Siamese safely inside.

A test can confirm a cat's FIV status as positive or negative. It's a good idea to have all breeding animals and all new cats coming into your household tested for FIV (and FeLV) to ensure their negative status, before exposing them to your Siamese.

The disease is incurable, although an infected cat may remain in relatively good health for months or years before its immune system weakens enough to allow secondary infections to take hold. Symptoms vary but usually include lethargy, weight loss, gum disease, and chronic infections.

The first vaccine for FIV became available in 2002, but its use remains controversial. Veterinarians do not typically recommend it, except for cats that regularly roam outdoors, because it results in a positive test for the virus, regardless of the cat's health status.

Vaccine Reactions

Although vaccines are considered highly effective weapons against several major feline diseases, they are not foolproof. Sometimes they fail to provide the necessary protection, although fortunately, this is uncommon. Side effects also occur, but these, too, are minimal in most cases. Many cats will experience mild lethargy for a day or two after receiving their shots, and this is generally no cause for concern. However, some vaccine reactions can be serious, causing a range of symptoms, including convulsions, vomiting, diarrhea, wheezing, restlessness, itching, labored breathing, swelling of the head and face, and even death. An allergic-type reaction can occur within 15 minutes to several hours after injection. Vaccine reactions are considered a true medical emergency, requiring immediate and aggressive veterinary treatment.

If your Siamese ever experiences an adverse vaccine reaction, be sure to report it, no matter how mild. To help ensure your cat's safety and comfort the next time, your veterinarian may recommend premedicating your Siamese to minimize the severity of any reaction.

Vaccine-induced tumors: Some cats seem to be more sensitive to certain vaccines than others. A particularly serious problem some cats experience is associated mostly with vaccines for feline leukemia virus (FeLV) and rabies. Cancerous tumors, called *fibrosarcomas*, may develop at the injection sites and end up being fatal most of the time. The suspected cause is not thought to be the vaccine itself, but something in the vaccine suspension or *adjuvant*. Currently, a nonadjuvant rabies vaccination is available, but it is approved only as a yearly vaccine, rather than three years.

As the problem continues to be researched, this is the main reason why veterinarians recommend FeLV vaccination only for cats at greatest risk of contracting the disease. Also, veterinarians avoid giving the FeLV vaccine between the shoulder blades because the tumors are less operable there. In an effort to standardize vaccine sites, and thus help track adverse reactions, the FeLV injection is now generally given in the cat's left rear leg, while the rabies vaccination is given in the right rear leg.

Diet-related Illness

Feline lower urinary tract disease (FLUTD), also known as feline urologic syndrome (FUS), is a potentially life-threatening condition caused by tiny mineral crystals that form in the cat's urinary tract, resulting in painful irritation and sometimes serious blockages. Although the problem can occur in both sexes, male cats are more prone to crystal blockages than females. This is because the tube that carries urine out of the body, the *urethra*, is longer and more narrow in males.

An afflicted cat may repeatedly lick its penis or vulva and urinate in unusual places, such as the bathtub. Feeling an uncomfortable urgency to urinate, the cat may make frequent trips to the litter box. It even may strain or cry as it attempts to void. Some people mistake this straining for constipation. If you notice these symptoms, or if you see blood in the urine, take your Siamese to a veterinarian immediately.

If the crystals block the urethra so that the cat cannot eliminate its urine, the kidneys may sustain irreversible damage from the backup pressure. Within a short time, toxic wastes can build up in the blood with fatal consequences. With prompt medical treatment, most cats recover; however, recurrences are common.

Dietary factors are closely associated with this illness. Years ago, research clearly implicated a connection between FLUTD and high magnesium levels in dry feline diets. As a result, pet food manufacturers reformulated their foods to help promote better urinary tract health (see page 38). They also began adding acidifying ingredients to their foods when it was learned that a slightly acidic urine, or low urine pH, helped dissolve the mineral waste crystals or prevented them from forming

Observe and know your cat's normal litter box habits. Any sudden change in elimination habits can be a sign of illness.

For safety's sake, store household cleaners and chemicals in cabinets behind closed doors, and keep your Siamese out of them.

in the first place. A higher (more alkaline) urine pH seems to favor crystal development.

Minor Problems and Illnesses

The serious infectious diseases of cats can be avoided or minimized by immunizations. Even so, there will fall into the life of every Siamese a certain amount of minor problems and illnesses. Stomach upsets and skin problems top the list. (Sounds very human, doesn't it?) If the minor stomach upset is the result of hair balls, eating too much, the wrong thing (short of poisonous substances), or too fast, there is usually nothing to worry about. Cats vomit very easily. The only remaining problem is getting the spot out of the carpet if you use food containing dyes.

Skin Problems

Most people think of skin problems as insignificant. While the majority of skin diseases are not life-threatening, they should not be neglected. If your Siamese develops a skin lesion, take it to the veterinarian. It could be something as minor as a fungal infection, which is usually self-limiting, but it also could be a condition that will worsen if untreated or, more importantly, may be a symptom of an internal problem. At the very least, consider that these conditions are unsightly and probably very uncomfortable for the cat. Most skin lesions are caused by fungus, allergies, or parasites.

Ringworm: The fungal infection commonly called ringworm is one of the few diseases that can be transmitted from cat to human and human to cat. Fungal spores are everywhere, and ringworm can break out with no known contact with another infected person or cat. Fortunately,

A healthy kitten is alert, curious, and bright-eyed.

in most cases—cat and human—it cures itself within six or seven weeks. Even so, it is not advisable to leave it untreated because of the possibility that it will become chronic and that it could be passed to others. It is first noticed when a patch of hair thins or falls out, but the infection has been underway for some time before this happens. As the fungus grows outward, the newly infected skin forms a reddened ring around the older, central part of the lesion, which is usually paler and scaly. There are many antifungal agents that can be used on cats. Your veterinarian should see the cat as soon as possible, make the diagnosis, and prescribe the treatment.

Allergies: The lesions caused by allergies may at first look like a fungus infection, but they are usually redder in the center than ringworm and may have a more irregular outline. Again, this is something that must be diagnosed and treated by a veterinarian. Cats can develop allergies to foods, parasites, and inhalants that will cause dermatitis. If food allergy is suspected, the veterinarian may recommend an elimination diet— taking away one type of food at a time—or a diet of food that the cat has never been exposed to before, such as lamb. (For allergies to develop there must have been an earlier exposure to the substance, the allergen.)

Parasites: If fleas have been around, your Siamese could develop flea-allergy dermatitis, which is the most common allergic skin disease in cats. There are several forms in which it may appear, including excessive grooming to the point of wearing the hair down to a stubble, red and elevated hairless areas on the abdomen or back of the hind legs, and a few to hundreds of tiny, crusty bumps either over the entire body or mostly on the head, back, and base of the tail. Obviously, if your Siamese has flea-allergy dermatitis, the fleas have to go. Your veterinarian will be able to advise you about the safest means of banishing fleas and may also want to treat your cat with corticosteroids to give immediate, but temporary, relief.

Allergic–inhalant dermatitis: Allergic-inhalant dermatitis is much less common than flea-allergy dermatitis and food allergies, but produces much the same symptoms. Pollens are the culprits here and strangely enough do not usually produce respiratory symptoms with the dermatitis.

Chin acne: Siamese especially are prone to a condition of the chin skin commonly known as chin acne. The hair follicles become clogged, bacteria grow, and the area looks dirty because of the resultant black particles. The chin is one of the most difficult places for the cat to groom. It does so by washing its paw as it holds it near the chin. A less than thorough cleansing allows bacteria to multiply. Keeping food off the chin is the first order of business: feed wet food in flat dishes, not bowls. If your cat gets chin acne, scrub the skin daily with soap and water, rinse well, and dry with a tissue or paper towel.

Stud tail: A skin problem usually confined to whole (unaltered) adult males is stud tail. An accumulation of a waxy secretion at the upper surface of the base of the tail can produce clogged pores and loss of hair. If not cleaned, the skin may become inflamed and infected. At the first signs—stiff, sticky hair—treat as recommended for chin acne: clean, rinse, and dry. Once the skin becomes infected, it is very hard to clear up.

Ear Mites

Ear mites are microscopic arthropods that affect the skin of the external ear, living off the cerumen (ear wax) and irritating the skin. The irritation causes an increase in production of cerumen. The ears become inflamed and clotted with excess cerumen. An ear mite infestation should not be neglected. The mites torment the cat with itching, so that it shakes its head and scratches at its ears: if left untreated, this can lead to hematomas in the ear. The hematomas can cause permanent damage to the delicate cartilage of the external ear, resulting in a crumpled, squashed ear. Do not attempt to clean the ears yourself if your Siamese displays any of the symptoms of ear mite infestation. Instead, seek prompt veterinary care. These days, the condition is much more easily remedied that it was once upon a time, when messy treatments had to be repeated over a two- or three-week period. Newer medications allow one-time treatment that effectively rids the ears of the itchy pests.

Eye Problems

Conjunctivitis, inflammation of the membrane that lines the eyelids and the exposed surface of the eye, can be caused by any number of irritants, mechanical and chemical, allergens, and pathogens, and is usually a minor problem, with the exception of the last-mentioned cause.

Again, minor does not mean that the problem can be ignored. The susceptibility of Siamese to eye irritations seems more pronounced in the lilac points, perhaps because of their higher degree of albinism. Tekena, a lilac-point female that was shown in the seventies, never went to a show without her bottle of feline eyewash because of the heavy pall of cigarette smoke in the show halls. Even with frequent eyewashes, her lids became red and the third eyelid, the nictitating membrane, extended. Fortunately, with fewer smokers among the exhibitors and smoking banned in most show halls, this is no longer a problem for show Siamese.

Irritants: Irritations such as those caused by smoke or allergens usually disappear with the removal of the offending substance from the environment of the Siamese. However, the condition can become chronic, especially if it is allowed to persist without an attempt at relieving the situation right away. The main problem with this is not the unsightliness of goopy eyes, nor the discomfort the cat may be enduring, but the possibility of infections developing in this compromised tissue. Infections may lead to swelling of the conjunctiva, elevation of the third eyelid, a yellowish discharge, and sensitivity to light, which causes the cat to squint. If not treated, the infection may produce a cloudiness over the eye. An infection this advanced can cause a corneal ulcer (keratitis), which, if not treated, can become a hole in the eye. The fluid inside the eye, which helps give the eyeball its

shape, can escape and pathogens can enter the interior of the eye. At this point, matters become very serious, with the partial loss of vision or the loss of the whole eye distinct possibilities.

Conjunctivitis: Conjunctivitis may also be an early sign of some diseases, such as feline viral rhinotracheitis (FVR). Whatever the cause, red, runny eyes should not be neglected. The chances are very high that the conjunctivitis will be minor, lasting just a few days and leaving no permanent damage, but increase the chances of a happy outcome by taking your Siamese to the veterinarian promptly and following her or his directions faithfully.

Treatment: Even with veterinary attention and prescribed medication, eye infections can worsen. One of the reasons is that the medication is rapidly washed out of the eye by tears and must be replaced every few hours. Well, if you've never put medicine in the sore eyes of a Siamese, you have a real treat in store. Siamese can turn themselves into pretzels, back off the edge of tables while their neck skin is in a vise-like grip, and generally go berserk when faced

Applying eye medication. This position leaves the hands free to control the head position and to put the drops or ointment into the trough between the eye and the lower lid.

Your cat is less likely to acquire internal parasites if you don't allow it outdoors to hunt and eat wild prey.

with eyedrops or ointment. My most successful method of doing it alone sounds difficult but really is not.

✔ Kneel on the floor and sit back on your heels.

✔ Wedge the patient's body, with its head facing forward (away from you), between your knees.

✔ One hand can be used to tilt the cat's head up slightly and, if the cat is struggling to escape, grip the neck skin between palm and last two fingers. The other hand is free to administer the medication.

✔ If the medication is in liquid form, just hold the bottle above the eye and let the drops fall in. If it is an ointment, squeeze a small amount onto the thumb side of your index finger and, with a rolling motion, deliver the ointment into the trough between the eye and the lower lid. (You may have to pull the lower lid down a bit with the index finger of the other hand.) Of course, if there are two or three people to help, it is much easier.

Joking aside, not medicating frequently enough is a great temptation, especially when Sammi hides when she hears the cap come off the tube and regards you with tearful, hurt eyes afterward. Think of the possibilities of a prolonged infection, which could lead to chronic conjunctivitis, or a more serious infection, which could require months of treatment, much of it at your hands, and stick to the medication schedule.

Internal Parasites

Worms: Internal parasites of cats consist mostly of worms. There are feline heartworms, eyeworms, and lungworms, but these are rare compared to the worms of the digestive tract. The intestinal parasites in cats are usually roundworms and flatworms. Several species of roundworms (nematodes) can infest cats, including ascarids, hookworm, and whipworm, with ascarids being the most common. Roundworms have complex life cycles that may

*Siamese are inquisitive to a fault and must
be kept away from poisonous plants.*

*Keep fish bowls and aquariums covered,
unless you want your Siamese to go "fishing."*

Two cats can become best buddies and keep each other company while you're away from home.

The tapeworm life cycle. The flea carries the microscopic larvae, which can be transmitted to the cat by a flea bite. The larvae migrate to the intestine and develop into a flat strand of segments, which absorbs nutrients from the contents of the intestine.

Flat worms include tapeworms and flukes. Flukes, which can infest lungs, liver, and intestines, are rare in housecats and usually come from eating raw fish. Much more common in cats are tapeworms, which lie in the intestine—to which they attach by one end, the scolex—and soak up the digested food. Segments (proglottids) are continually produced from the region just behind the scolex, forming a long ribbon. At the other end of the ribbon, the segments, which are loaded with fertilized eggs, break off and make their way out of the cat's anus. At this stage they look like grains of cooked rice and may creep about, carrying what are now embryos. The proglottid dies and disintegrates; the embryos are eaten by flea and lice larvae, which can then pass them on to their hosts. If you find a flea on your Siamese, wait two or three weeks to give the tapeworm larvae time to get to the digestive tract, and then have your veterinarian give it a appropriate treatment. Before a medication called Droncit was discovered, tapeworm treatment consisted of a substance that caused intestinal contractions that were painful to the cat and usually left the scolex in place. Droncit affects the cuticle of the tapeworm, the outer covering that normally protects it from the cat's digestive juices, and the whole worm is digested. This compound is very effective and need be given only once, unless Sammi picks

involve more than one host animal. The adults lie in the intestine and absorb nutrients from the cat's food or tap into small intestinal arteries. They lay eggs, which pass out of the body with the feces. In some species, the eggs are ingested by and develop in other animals, such as rodents and insects. A cat can become infected by eating an infected mouse or beetle. In other species, the eggs, which can survive for years, are ingested by the cat without an intermediate host. The eggs develop into larvae that migrate through the lungs of the cat, causing a cough or even pneumonia. The larvae can also be passed to kittens through the milk of an infected queen. Infestation is more serious for kittens than adults, but in both may cause vomiting and diarrhea. Sometimes, roundworms can be seen in the vomit or feces. Fortunately, they can be eliminated from cats by careful hygiene, keeping the cat from walking on grass and soil, preventing it from capturing and eating prey, making sure that it eats only cooked meats, and having a veterinarian prescribe a course of treatment.

Health and condition. The healthy Siamese is sleek and smooth, neither bony nor flabby. The sick Siamese may have an "open" coat, loose skin, and look very uncomfortable. The very ill Siamese often lies in an elbows-up position.

up another flea. That's why effective flea control prevents tapeworm infestations.

The final caution about minor problems and diseases is that they have the potential to become major and should never be neglected.

Potentially Serious Symptoms

This section could be titled "When to Call the Veterinarian," but I have already advised you to call the veterinarian whenever anything looks amiss. The following are symptoms that absolutely cannot be ignored, although some of them may not necessarily indicate a serious illness.

✔ Bleeding, from a wound or any body opening
✔ Difficulty in breathing, usually with the neck extended and mouth open
✔ Repeated vomiting and/or diarrhea
✔ Refusal to eat and drink
✔ Extreme lassitude and nonresponsiveness
✔ Seizures
✔ Pupils unresponsive to light or different from each other
✔ Inability to maintain normal posture
✔ Lameness or inability to walk normally
✔ Signs of disorientation, such as walking in circles or bumping into objects
✔ Difficulty in giving birth
✔ Difficulty in urinating or any sudden changes in litter box habits
✔ Unexpected weight loss

✔ Increase in fluid intake and output (urine)
✔ Lumps and swellings, particularly of the abdomen
✔ Abdominal tenderness
✔ Persistent cough, wet or dry
✔ A general appearance of illness—uncomfortable looking, coat open, elbows up, distant gaze

The implications of these various symptoms are too many to describe here. Some are quite obvious. All of them should be taken very seriously, and the occurrence of any one of them should result in an immediate call to your veterinarian.

FELINE REPRODUCTION

While breeding cats should be left to professionals, every Siamese owner needs a basic knowledge of feline reproduction and genetics to fully appreciate the breed. Otherwise, be a responsible pet owner and spay or neuter your Siamese.

Feline Mating Rituals and Reproduction

If you're going to own a cat, it helps to know how it came into the world. Some familiarity with feline mating rituals and reproduction will enhance your overall knowledge and understanding of cats and their behavior.

Sexual Maturity

First, let's talk terminology. An intact (not spayed) female cat is called a *queen*. An intact (not neutered) male is called a *tom* or *stud*. Although her first heat cycle (estrus) may occur as early as six months of age, a queen should be allowed to reach full maturity (at least one year old) before she is bred. A tom reaches sexual maturity between 9 and 14 months, and from then on, his hormones rule his life.

Spaying and neutering make Siamese better household companions, because they no longer feel the biological urge to roam in search of mates.

His sex hormones also trigger his instinctive urge to spray and mark his territory with strong-smelling urine. Thankfully, neutering usually curbs this disgusting tomcat trait, which is good reason to alter as soon as is advisable.

Estrus

A queen comes into heat or estrus according to seasonal rhythms, usually starting in early spring. Feline reproductive cycles appear to be triggered by 12 or more hours of daylight per day. Most queens cycle every two or three weeks during the breeding season; others cycle only once a month, with many exceptions in between. Cats are, after all, highly individualistic about everything they do.

A few queens have *silent* heats, but for most of them, there's no mistaking when they're in season. The hallmark signs include increased restlessness and vocal calling. The queen may seem more affectionate toward her owners, rubbing against them and wanting to be petted. She may roll on the ground or pace from door to door, waiting for any opportunity to escape

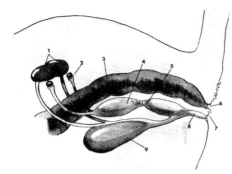

The female urogenital system.

1. *kidney*   6. *anus*
2. *ovaries*   7. *vulva*
3. *large intestine* 8. *vagina*
4. *uterus*   9. *bladder*
5. *cervix*

outdoors. The queen's persistent calling advertises her availability to the neighborhood toms, which prowl nearby, lured by her sounds and sex pheromones. After a night or two of their incessant, nerve-wracking caterwauling, most people are easily convinced to cart their queen off to the veterinarian's for spay surgery.

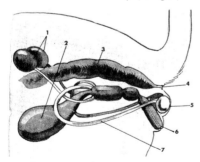

The male urogenital system.

1. *kidney*   5. *testicles*
2. *bladder*   6. *penis*
3. *large intestine* 7. *vas deferens*
4. *anus*

Induced Ovulation

Female cats are unusual in that they do not ovulate spontaneously, as many mammal species do; instead, ovulation is induced by copulation. The male's penis is ridged with tiny spines or barbs that scrape the inside of the queen's vagina during copulation, which is, no doubt, why the mating act ends with a howling roar from the female. This physical stimulation apparently sends a message along nerve pathways to areas in the brain that release luteinizing hormone, a chemical that prompts the release of eggs from the ovaries.

Timing, as in everything, is critical. Research indicates that the most critical time in the heat cycle is the third through the fourth day. Several matings on these days are needed to trigger the hormonal changes that bring about ovulation and prepare the uterine lining for implantation.

The Mating Ritual

With Siamese, the sex act is hardly a quiet affair, as one might expect, since the breed is so well known for vocalizations.

✔ The male usually sits very tall and sings to the female first.

✔ She may roll on the floor or the couch.

✔ When the male sees his opportunity, he will lunge for the back of her neck and take a mouthful of the loose (and tough) skin there.

✔ Her response is to crouch low and move her tail to one side.

✔ The male then steps on one of her thighs repeatedly, which causes the female to elevate her hindquarters and allows completion of the mating.

✔ As the acts ends, the female lets out a roar and a howl.

Proper Nutrition in Pregnancy

Proper nutrition is vital for the queen's health and for the developing fetuses. Because her protein needs will increase dramatically, she should be fed a cat food specifically formulated and labeled for feline growth and reproduction.

The pair usually mate several more times. If the queen is bred and becomes pregnant, gestation normally lasts an average 65 or 66 days, although this may vary somewhat from queen to queen.

Signs of Pregnancy

Usually the first signs of pregnancy are a pinking and enlargement of the nipples at three to four weeks. Sometimes the queen will have morning sickness, vomiting a small amount of clear stomach fluid before breakfast, within a week or so. At 16 to 30 days the embryos in their membranes are like little balls at intervals in the uterus. At this time they can be palpated (felt), but this should be done *only* by a veterinarian and *only* for a good reason. Before this time, the fetuses are too small to be felt, and later they elongate and fill the uterine horns like stuffed sausages and are difficult to distinguish from one another until after 45 days or so. The caution about any palpation is not because of the difficulty of feeling the kittens, but because

Sexing kittens. The male, on left; the female, on the right.

of the real danger of damaging the uterus or kittens. Also for this reason, children should not be allowed to pick up or handle a pregnant cat.

Final Weeks of Pregnancy

A noticeable change in the queen's girth may not occur until rather late in the pregnancy—six weeks or so, depending to some extent on the number of kittens. While the developing kittens, called fetuses from 28 days to birth, have all their organs at four weeks, they are only 1 inch (2.5 cm) long. At five to six weeks they are about 2½ inches (6 cm) long.

Birth

Once labor commences, kittens start to arrive about 15 to 30 minutes apart in most cases, although this can vary. About half of all kittens arrive head first; the other half emerge hind feet and tail end first. Each kitten emerges either completely or partially enclosed in a grayish, semitransparent bubble, called the *amniotic sac* or *placental membrane*. Most experienced queens will instinctively strip this sac away, sever the umbilical cords, and force-

Female Siamese in heat tend to be quite vocal.

which includes playing Mama Cat and massaging their tiny bottoms with a warm, damp washcloth to stimulate elimination.

A healthy newborn weighs on average 3 or 4 ounces (about 100 g) and begins gaining weight rapidly in a couple of days. A day or two after birth, the umbilical stumps dry and falls off the newborns. In about 10 days, the kittens' eyes begin to open. At first, all kittens' eyes are blue, whether Siamese or not. Eye color changes to their adult shade at about 12 weeks of age. By 15 to 20 days old, kittens start crawling. Soon afterward, they begin to stand and toddle.

Color

Siamese are born white. Near the end of the first week the very first color begins to show in the Siamese kitten's new hairs growing along the edges of the ears, the coolest area. Seal and blue points usually color in first, followed by chocolate point, and last, lilac point. In the second week the fur on the trail will take on a tinge of color, although it will still be difficult to be certain of the point color, if more than one is genetically possible in the litter. Color begins to come on the tip of the nose, too. Even so, it might be weeks more before one can be certain what color a kitten will be.

Socialization

Experts say that kittens socialized to humans at an early age grow up to be better-adjusted, people-oriented pets. That's why good breeders make it a point to gently handle their kittens a little each day beginning at about three weeks of age. This helps them get used to the human touch.

fully lick each kitten clean to stimulate its breathing and circulation. In most cases, the entire litter arrives within two to six hours, although this, too, may vary.

Kitten Development

Healthy kittens begin suckling just minutes after birth. It's important that they nurse right away so they can ingest disease-fighting antibodies contained in the mother's first milk, called the *colostrum*. Born with eyes and ears closed, each kitten selects its own nipple and tends to stay with that one for the first week or so; later they nurse on any of them.

After each meal, the mother licks the kittens' genitals to make them urinate and defecate. Most people do not realize that newborn kittens cannot evacuate on their own. Many a breeder has been faced with the grueling task of hand-raising and bottle-feeding kittens,

Caution: Suspending a kitten by its neck skin without supporting the rear end with your other hand can cause serious nerve damage and paralysis. The queen may drag her kittens around by the nape of the neck, but when she wants to travel, she picks one up by the whole neck, which fits without harm across her partially closed mouth in the gap between her canines and premolars. Since humans can't do this, we must use *two* hands.

Speaking of hands, do not let your kitten play with your hands. Use a toy as an extension of yourself instead. And do not play roughly with your kitten. Kittens that are taught to play rough with humans will grow into cats that cannot be petted without the danger of a painful play attack.

Litter Box Training

At one month, kittens begin to play with each other, engaging in mock chase and combat games intended to hone their hunting skills. Also by this time, they can control their own elimination, and litter box training can begin.

The first litter pan should be kitten-size, shallow enough for short legs to easily access. Contrary to popular belief, the queen does not teach her kittens to use the litter box. This behavior is an instinct that is switched on sometime around the weaning period. Basically, all you have to do is provide the litter pan and show the kitten where it is. The kitten usually figures out the rest in due time.

Weaning

Usually around four to six weeks, kittens begin sampling soft, solid foods. This is the beginning of a gradual weaning process as the kittens shift

---

═══ TIP ═══

Handling a Kitten

There are two cautions about handling a kitten: Never pick one up by the scruff of the neck, and never roughhouse with one. If the kitten is too big to fit in your hand, put one hand under its chest, with your forefinger directed forward between its front legs and your thumb and remaining fingers curving up around either side and behind the front legs. At the same time, place your other hand under its hindquarters.

---

from nursing to eating on their own. By about 6 or 8 weeks, kittens are, in most cases, fully weaned and ready to leave their mother. However, most breeders of purebred cats will not release their kittens to new homes until 12 to 16 weeks of age. This allows the kitten to gain some maturity so it can better adjust to new surroundings. It also allows time for the breeder to get in at least one round of vaccinations before the kitten goes to its new home.

Registration

At two months of age, a kitten's point colors should be evident, so it is time to be registered. There are two stages of registration: litter registration, which the breeder handles, and individual registration, which the new owner completes. Depending on the terms of the sale, the breeder may sell the registration papers with the kitten or choose to withhold them until the new owner produces proof that the kitten has been spayed or neutered.

On the individual registration form, the breeder completes the section for the kitten's sex, breed, eye color, coat color, and so forth. If the breeder has a cattery name, it will be printed on the line where the new owner writes in the name chosen for the kitten. The cattery name becomes part of your cat's registered name.

When a registry receives the form with the appropriate fee, it will verify the pedigree information, approve a name selection, and then send the buyer an official owner's certificate.

Basic Genetics

Coat color and pattern in the Siamese cat are the result of the interaction of several different genes and the environment. Just as in humans, cats inherit one set of chromosomes from each parent through the fusion of an egg cell, which has one of each kind of chromosome from the mother, and a sperm cell, which has one of each kind from the father. The new individual thus has a double set of chromosomes, as did its parents. These chromosomes provide for its development as a cat instead of a rat, as well as its individual inherited characteristics, such as eye color, coat length, and coat color.

A gene is a linear portion of a chromosome that is responsible for the way a certain cell product is put together by the cell's metabolic machinery. Since all the cells of an individual, with the exception of its gametes (sperm or egg cells), have a double set of chromosomes, all of these cells have two of each kind of gene.

A gene may undergo a change such that it becomes different enough from the original form of the gene to make a detectable difference in its cell product. This is called a *mutation*. The original form of the gene is called the *wild type* and the new form is the *mutant*. Additional mutations can produce even more different forms of that one gene. All the different forms of a gene are called its *alleles*.

Homozygosity: When both copies of a certain gene are identical in information, that is, they consist of the same allele, we say that the individual is homozygous for whatever trait is governed by that gene.

Heterozygosity: This term describes the situation in which an individual has two different alleles for a certain gene. The allele that expresses itself even when present in only one copy is the "dominant" one; the other allele's expression will not be evident unless the individual is homozygous for this "recessive" allele.

Restriction of Color

Now, let us relate all of this to the basic coat pattern of the Siamese with its acromelanism, the restriction of color to the extremities. The explanation for this strange pattern is actually very simple: a mutation occurred in one of the genes that provide for the various enzymes needed for the production of pigment. The mutation resulted in an enzyme that was less firmly held together in its three-dimensional shape than the wild type enzyme; because of this, when the mutant enzyme is subjected to temperatures of approximately 98°F (37°C) and above, it unfolds a bit, losing that critical shape and thereby losing the ability to catalyze its step in the pathway to pigment. If the cells of the hair root are at that temperature or above, little or no pigment will be made and placed in the growing hair; if they are at a temperature below that, the mutant enzyme keeps its shape and functions in the production of pigment, producing pigmented hair. In the Siamese, only the skin of the "points"—face (mask), ears, feet, and tail—is cool enough for the mutant enzyme to work. The skin of the neck and body is normally too warm and very little pigment is made there. Because this mutation limits the amount of pigment formed, it is considered a case of partial albinism.

This is a good place to speak again of homozygosity and heterozygosity. If a cat is heterozygous for the gene under consideration, each of its cells will have a copy of the mutant allele and a copy of the wild type allele. Since the wild type allele will provide for wild type enzyme, which is unimpaired by the normal range of body temperatures, there will be pigment in the hair all over the body. Because we can see the effect of the wild type allele even when paired with the mutant allele, whose effect cannot be seen, we say that the wild type is dominant to the mutant in this case. Only when a cat is homozygous for the mutant form, that is, when both alleles are the mutant form, will the effect of the mutation be evident, resulting in a cat with acromelanism, the Siamese or pointed coat.

Actually, studies of this coat pattern were first conducted and published using a breed of rabbit called Himalayan, which also shows pigment restriction to the points. Experimenters produced pigmented patches on Himalayan rabbits by strapping small ice packs to their backs for a time. Similarly, Siamese that stay outside in cold weather will turn dark all over. Conversely, if part of a point of a Himalayan rabbit or a Siamese cat is made warmer, the new hair there will be unpigmented. Experiments on Siamese cats were done by two Russian geneticists, N. A. and V. N. Iljin, who reported in 1930 in *The Journal of Heredity* the effects of both keeping Siamese in a cold environment and of bandaging a shaved area over the shoulders. The cold environment resulted in a darkening of the normally light-colored body. The bandage added warmth to the underlying shaved skin, which then produced unpigmented fur.

Color Variations

Natural changes in skin temperature will also upset the normal pattern. A very obese Siamese will have a darker body coat because the extra fat under the skin insulates the skin from the underlying body and its heat, making the skin cool enough to produce pigment. A respiratory illness, with its inflammation of the membranes of the nose and sinuses, produces an elevated temperature in the skin of the face. The hair that is growing at that time will be unpigmented, and, in a week or so, as it emerges, will give the mask a grizzled look.

Because the pigment-producing cells are also affected by certain hormones, there may be coloration changes brought about by changing length of days, which is detected by the nervous system, which in turn affects the endocrine system, and by pregnancy. Whatever the cause of these natural variations, the stunning contrast of dark and light coat will be regained after the tubby Siamese has slimmed down, the kittens are weaned, or the fever is a dim memory.

In addition to the gene determining whether the color is solid all over (self) or restricted to the points (acromelanism), there are other genes that alter the molecular composition of the pigment and the way the pigment molecules are clumped into granules in the cells. These changes affect the way that the pigment in the hair shaft interacts with light and thus what color the hair appears to us. The interaction of these various genes produces the various point colors and patterns of the Siamese cat.

GROOMING

The healthy Siamese requires little in the way of grooming. However, that little is important and should be done with as little fuss as possible. Get your Siamese used to being groomed while it's a kitten.

Head

Eyes

Starting at the front, the eyes may become irritated by smoke or allergens, resulting in the production of mucus, which dries in the corners of the eyes. These dried secretions can be removed with a tissue, but you may have to immobilize the cat to do so. Cats hate having anything done to their eyes. My method is to kneel on the floor with the cat facing outward between my knees; then, one hand can hold the head and pull down on the lower eyelid while the other wields the tissue or applies eyedrops or ointment.

Ears

Next, the ears. Ears, even when healthy, need to be cleaned from time to time. How often varies from cat to cat. If brown secretions are visible in the ears, arm yourself with many cotton balls and clean. Dampen a cotton ball with

The large ears and wedge-shaped face are desirable features in show-quality Siamese.

water and swab away. *Never poke anything down inside the ear.*

Chin

On Siamese the chin seems particularly susceptible to a condition known as chin acne. This has been described earlier, on page 58. The best preventive for this is a clean chin. If your Siamese is lax in washing its chin, scrub its chin with plain soap and water and rinse well.

Teeth and Gums

Some Siamese, as they get older, develop gum disease. Brushing their teeth may help prevent this by removing plaque before it hardens into tartar. This is definitely one of those things that is easier said than done. There are various techniques, but the ones I have found easiest to manage are a dry, cotton-tipped swab or a fingertip with a 2-inch-square (5-cm^2) scrap of thin terrycloth. The best I can do is the outer surfaces, but I have heard of cats that also allow the inner surfaces to be done. Do not use toothpaste for humans as some of it contains compounds that are dangerous to cats, and trying to rinse a cat's mouth after brushing really makes the whole experience burdensome, if not impossible.

Nails

Nails must be clipped every two to three weeks. Even with scratching posts to help pull off the old, outer sheaths of nail, further help in the form of clipping is needed. Pick a time when the Siamese is relaxed. Gently press on the top of each toe to cause the nail to extend. Using a nail clipper or cat nail scissors, clip off the white portion of each nail. Stay away from the pink area; that is the "quick." Some Siamese are very tolerant of this procedure. If yours is not, you may need to enlist a pedicure partner. While you wield the clippers, have the partner pinch the neck skin of the Siamese, without pulling upward. This evokes the "freeze" response of kittenhood and gives you more wiggle-free time to do the job.

Combing and Brushing

Aside from bathing (see HOW-TO, page 78), a more common and less traumatic form of coat grooming is simply combing or brushing, with none of that wet stuff around. A pocket comb will do for clearing the coat of loose hairs; simply comb with the direction of hair growth—from head to tail. Most cats enjoy this. Slightly damp hands can accomplish the same thing, but you must first rub the fur backward, from tail to head, and then head to tail.

For special purposes, special grooming aids are called for. There are many pet combs and brushes available. Do not use wire brushes on Siamese; they are designed for the heavier coats and larger bodies of dogs. If you suspect your Siamese has fleas, there are small, metal flea combs that can be used on cats and that are effective in capturing fleas. Use short strokes in the direction of hair growth, and, when the fleas are caught, dunk the comb into a bowl of soapy water where the fleas will come out of the comb and be drowned.

Human hair brushes will not do much for a cat's coat, but there are solid rubber brushes for cats that will. These are about the size and shape of a nail brush. One side of the brush has a flat bed of hundreds of quarter-inch-long, fingerlike projections. This side is used to clear loose hairs from the coat by ordinary brushing strokes from head to tail. My Siamese line up for this and never seem to get enough of it. The base of the other side of the brush is cut into a shallow V and covered with shorter projections. This side is used with a short, scooping motion—again, in the direction of hair growth, and will remove not only loose hairs but some that are not. The effect is to thin the coat, but excessive use could make scanty or bald spots in the coat.

Tail

And finally, we come to the end of the cat and the one place the Siamese most welcomes grooming assistance—its tail tip. It seems that tail tips are difficult to wash, perhaps because they are at the end of those long, flexible tails and can be washed in one direction only—tipward. Years ago I discovered that if you hold the tail about one inch (2.5 cm) from the tip and present it to the Siamese, it will scrub it vigorously in every direction (as they do their body fur), happily leaving it a bushy, but clean, mess!

Flea Control

No discussion of grooming and coat care would be complete without a discussion of flea control. Fleas are one of the most common grooming problems pet owners encounter. Easy to spot, these annoying insects leave behind evidence of their visits to the host in the form of *flea dirt*, which looks like fine grains of black sand or pepperlike granules in the cat's fur. Rub your hand against the fur along the cat's back and near the neck and tail and inspect the skin for tiny black specks. If you see any, your Siamese has fleas.

Fleas feed on your cat's blood. The tiny black specks are flea excrement from digested blood, deposited in your cat's fur. When dampened, the specks dissolve into bloody smudges. Left untreated, flea infestations can cause anemia from blood loss, especially in kittens, and damage a cat's coat and skin from excessive scratching.

Even indoor cats are not immune to the scourge of fleas. The tiny, bloodthirsty creatures will jump through window screens or ride in on a person's clothing or shoes in search of a suitable, warm-blooded host. Once indoors, fleas lay eggs on the host (your Siamese) and turn its fur into a factory for millions more. As the cat moves and scratches, the eggs fall off into your carpets, upholstery, and bedding, where they hatch into larvae. The larvae feed on debris among deep carpet fibers, an indoor environment that mimics their natural habitat—grass.

Treatment

Effective flea control used to require an expensive arsenal of products designed to treat the pet and its environment at various phases of the flea's complex life cycle. This arsenal

CHECKLIST

Flea Control Products

When choosing and using any type of flea control product on your Siamese, read the product label directions carefully before applying it. Remember these important rules:

1 Select only products that are *labeled as safe for use on cats.*

2 Do NOT use products intended for dogs as these may contain medications that are too strong, potentially even fatal, when applied to cats.

3 Never use any product on a kitten or a debilitated cat without first asking your veterinarian if it is safe to do so.

4 Be aware that some products do not mix well, so before using more than one flea control product, or before using any product with other medications your cat may be taking, ask your veterinarian if the ingredients can be used together safely.

included sprays, dips, powders, flea collars, medicated shampoos, and room foggers, all targeted to kill or control fleas at the egg, larval, pupal, or adult stages. Often, these products failed to be effective when applied during the wrong life cycle of the insect and required repeating. They could also be potentially dangerous if used inappropriately or in combination with incompatible products. Even flea collars, although easy to use, posed a risk of strangling or choking, unless designed with elastic or breakaway sections to make them safer.

One of the benefits of owning a shorthaired cat like the Siamese is that it requires only minimal grooming.

One-spot products: Thankfully, modern-day flea control is now much easier and more effective with the one-spot products that can be applied topically once a month for long-lasting control. Your veterinarian can recommend and dispense one of several brands currently on the market. These products typically come in a small tube and are dabbed directly onto the cat's skin at the back of the neck once a month. The active ingredient spreads across the entire animal and kills adult fleas by impairing the insects' nervous systems, before they can lay eggs and before they can bite and irritate the cat.

Get your Siamese accustomed to being groomed from an early age.

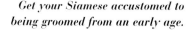

These lilac-point kittens have the sleekness and slender structure desired in show-quality Siamese.

Seal tortie points are almost always females. This one shows the pattern as shading on the body.

There are three basic ways to bathe a cat: the bucket method, the birdbath, and the shower. The trick is in discovering which is least frightening to your Siamese and thus the safest and easiest for all concerned. Whichever method you use, prepare everything—the room, the water, yourself—before bringing in the cat, whose nails were clipped the day before.

The Room

The room should be warm, draft-free, and wet-scared-cat-proof. Bathrooms are ideal.
- Remove all breakables.
- Loop shower and window curtains out of the way.
- Put out a face cloth, at least two bath towels, cat shampoo (mild, unscented hand-dishwashing liquid is good), and a bath mat or rug on which to kneel.

Water

The water should be the temperature of the cat's body, which is about 102°F (39°C). If you use a thermometer to check the water temperature, be sure to put it away before bringing in the Siamese.

Mental Preparation

Prepare yourself physically by removing all jewelry and wearing old, tough clothes. Mental preparation involves repeating to yourself a few hundred times: "I will be calm and determined, and all will go well."

Bucket Method

The bucket method calls for two, preferably three buckets, pails, or plastic wastebaskets. Rectangular ones fit better side by side in the bathtub than round ones. Fill each bucket with cat-temperature water to within 3 or 4 inches (7.6–10 cm) of the top. If you overfill them, the sound of the water spilling out as you put the cat in can be the last straw for an apprehensive cat. To the first bucket add a tablespoon of cat shampoo or the mild hand-dishwashing liquid, and mix. This will aid in wetting the cat's fur. The second and third buckets are for rinsing. Now bring in the bathee.

✔ If fleas are suspected, wet the cat's neck all around with the shampoo and work it in well before you start the bath. This keeps the fleas from going up to hide in the ears and facial fur when the rest of the cat is immersed.

✔ Hold the cat firmly as described before, one hand under the chest with a grip between and behind the arms and the other under the rump.

✔ Lower the cat slowly into the soapy water. Avoid splashing, which frightens most cats. The cat will probably grip the edge of the bucket, but will not be terribly upset with being in water if the water is

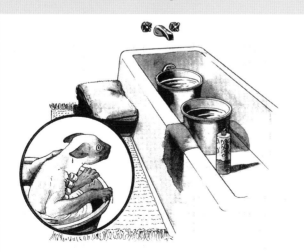

The two-bucket method of bathing. Be sure to have plenty of towels nearby.

at its body temperature and its face does not get splashed.

✔ Maintain the chest-arm grip and use the other hand to go through its fur, making sure that the water penetrates it.

✔ Lift the cat out, set it down in the tub, pour on more shampoo and work it into the coat, keeping that chest grip all the while. When the cleansing is done, immerse the cat in the first bucket once more, making sure to wet the neck well. This serves as a first rinse.

✔ Take the cat out and squeegee it with your free hand, going from the neck along the back to the end of the tail and down each leg. Repeat this rinsing and squeegeeing process through the second and third buckets.

Birdbath Method

The second method, the birdbath, is a modification of the bucket method. Instead of buckets, shallow containers, such as dishpans, are used. Again, rectangular ones work best. Cats that cannot be put into water up to their necks in buckets may be willing to stand in a few inches of water in a pan. The sequence is the same as for the bucket method, but getting the coat wet and clean all over is harder. A face cloth helps and is less splashy than scooping up water by hand to wet the cat.

Shower Method

The shower method requires a hand-held spray attachment for the bathtub faucet or the use of the kitchen sink, if it has a built-in sprayer. The water temperature must be adjusted carefully in advance and left turned on to a gentle spray. If the sprayer is held right against a cat's body it does not seem to frighten them. The sequence again is the same—wet, shampoo, rinse thoroughly, and squeegee off the excess water.

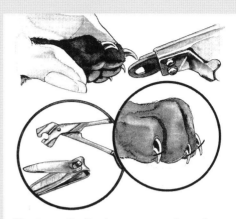

Clipping nails. Gently compress palm and knuckles to extend the claw. Cut below the quick using guillotine cutter, cat claw scissors, or nail clippers.

You may find that some combination of these methods works best for you and your Siamese. For example, you may be able to immerse it once, but there is no way it is going back into all that wet stuff up to its neck. In this case, a birdbath or shower finish will be considered not so bad and better tolerated.

After the last squeegeeing, wrap the cat in a towel with only its head out and hold it on your lap. Clean the ears with cotton-tipped swabs. If the face needs washing, use the corner of the face cloth. Be careful to avoid getting shampoo in its eyes. When the towel feels damp, change to a second one. Rub the fur every which way to further dry it. If necessary, use a third towel. Empty the buckets, wipe up the drips and spills, make a dry bed for the damp, angry Siamese, and leave it in the bathroom to rewash and dry itself (with its own little pink washcloth), while you prepare a special dinner for it. An extra serving of the offended one's favorite food soothes its nerves and mends the snag in the feline-human friendship.

Showing your Siamese can be fun and very educational, but it is not for everyone nor for every Siamese. Even if showing isn't for you, you'll learn a lot about cats by visiting shows as a spectator.

Visit Shows

Before deciding about showing your Siamese, it would be wise to visit a show or two and watch the goings-on. You will see a certain tension as the exhibitors (owners) take their cats to each of the judging areas, wait while their cat is judged, and then wait again to see if the cat is called back for the finals. Even the best cats do not make the top five in every final, so some disappointment is given. But for those who do not expect to place in every final and who enjoy the many other aspects of showing, the pleasures outweigh the pains.

Once you decide that you want to show your Siamese, you must familiarize yourself with the qualities expected of a show Siamese and determine whether yours is eligible to be shown. The first requirement is that your

The handsome and exotic lynx point has noticeable tabby striping on its legs and tail.

Siamese be registered or, at least, have registered parents.

Breed Standards

If your Siamese came from a breeder, ask the breeder to evaluate the show potential of your cat. Even if your Siamese is a kitten, the experienced breeder should be able to tell you whether it is likely to be show quality. Other valuable sources of information are the breed standards and show rules of the various cat registries (see Information). These cost only a few dollars and provide a wealth of information. The show rules describe the format of the shows sanctioned by that registry, the eligibility rules, the judging procedures, and much more. The breed standards include descriptions of every breed, including Siamese, of course, recognized by that organization. The Siamese breed standard will describe the ideal Siamese and the point allotment for each feature of the

---

TIP

Preparing for a Show

To prepare for a show requires some very down-to-earth information and an understanding of the ideal of the Siamese standard.

✔ The practical side includes making cage drapes of the correct dimensions (bath towels will do), arranging fasteners to hang them, fixing up a show kit of eyewash, cotton swabs, tissues, baby food, low-volume, high-calorie supplement as a treat, twist-ties or pipe cleaners to secure loose cage connections, and a favorite bed.

✔ A plastic cover for the top of the cage is useful in winter months.

---

cat. The total number of points for the ideal is 100, but even the winningest Siamese may be a point or two shy of perfection.

General Guidelines

Disqualifications

If you must evaluate your cat without assistance, here are some general guidelines. First, there are grounds for disqualification that apply to all breeds. Most of these are for physical conditions, including blindness, malocclusion, pregnancy, cryptorchidism (testicles not descended), an abnormal number of toes, and a lack of claws, but unruly behavior can also be a cause for disqualification if the cat cannot be handled by the judge even with the assistance of the owner. Altered (castrated, spayed) cats may be shown, but compete in their own division.

Faults

Then there are faults that are described for each breed. In the Siamese breed there are certain traits that are considered so undesirable that most organizations require that all wins be withheld (W/W) if the cat or kitten has any one of these: crossed eye, kinked tail, white spot, or eye color other than blue.

Condition

Finally, the ultimate test of your cat's show potential is the show ring itself. If your Siamese is registered or registerable, has none of the major faults above, is not excessively shy or frightened of strangers, and you want to give showing a try, enter a show and see what happens. But before you do anything else, be sure that your Siamese is eating a healthful diet (see the chapter, Nutrition, if in doubt), is free of internal and external parasites, and has no health problems. These things are absolute necessities for good general condition and a chance at winning in shows. Improving your cat's condition to show standards may take weeks, if it is overweight, for example, or months, if a deficient diet or disease has given it a rough, coarse coat.

Finding a Show

The next step is to locate shows in your area. Check the show calendars in the cat magazines and contact the cat registries. The registries may also give you a list of their clubs in your area, as individual clubs are usually the sponsors of the shows. Once you have found a show that is in your area, check the entry deadline. Shows usually close entries about one month before the date of the show. If the deadline is just past, call the entry clerk; there may be a chance of getting your entry in. If time is no problem, write or call the entry clerk for an entry blank and a show flyer, which gives basic information about the show. Be sure to indicate that you are a new exhibitor, as many clubs will provide extra information in advance and special assistance at the show.

Entering

The entry blank will look something like the form on this page.

The first several lines call for information that is on the cat's individual registration certificate. If your Siamese is registered with an association other than the one sanctioning the show, you will have to either register it with the show's association or supply registration numbers (from any registry) for its sire and dam, plus a small "listing" fee.

An agent is someone authorized to show the cat for you and need be designated only if you are not attending the show yourself. Sometimes exhibitors put in a fellow exhibitor's name just to be covered in case they have to leave the show hall for a time.

Category

The competition class can be confusing to the beginner.

• If your Siamese cannot be registered or for some other reason is ineligible for showing as a pedigreed cat, it could be shown as a household pet. In that case, under Household Pet you would check the SH for shorthair, and either Kitten, if it will be at least four months old but

Cat's Name	Color		Sex
Registration Number	Breed	Eye Color	Birthdate
Sire's Name	Registration number, if required		
Dam's Name	Registration number, if required		
Breeder	Agent		
Owner's Name	Telephone Number		
Owner's Address			

Competition Class

Household Pet	Nonchampionship
__ LH __ SH	__ Kitten
__ Kitten __ Adult	__ AOV
	__ Experimental Breed
Alter (Premier) Division	Championship Division
__ Novice	__ Novice
__ Champion (Premier)	__ Champion
__ Grand Champion (Premier)	__ Grand Champion

Special Benching Requests:

not yet eight months old on the day of the show, or Adult, if it will be eight months or older then.

• Most Siamese fit into one of the other categories. If your Siamese is eligible for show and will be at least four months old but not yet eight months old on the day of the show, check the Kitten blank under Nonchampionship.

• If the eligible Siamese will be eight months or older on the day of the show, has not

The seal point is the most common Siamese color seen at shows.

each other and socialize between judgings. As a new exhibitor, you could ask to be benched next to a club member or some other experienced exhibitor who would be willing to answer questions and show you the ropes.

Entry fee: The entry fee is given in the show calendar listing and on the show flyer. The fees vary, as they are based on the number of judging rings, which can be four to six in a one-day show and even more in a two- or three-day show. On the average, the range is $35 to $65. The fee must be sent (as a check or money order) with the completed and signed entry form to the entry clerk.

Confirmation

A confirmation of your entry will be sent to you shortly after the entry clerk receives the form and fee. If you do not receive a confirmation within two weeks, telephone the clerk. With the confirmation there will be further information about the show, including travel directions and the dimensions of the cages.

Grooming

Grooming of your Siamese is minimal. Unless they escape into the basement and get filthy, they need not be bathed. In fact, bathing will remove the natural oils in the coat and make it fluffy, which is highly undesirable. The nails on all the feet should be clipped. Some exhibitors trim the "ear furnishings"—the hair inside the ears—to enhance the size of the ears. A rubber brush is useful in removing loose hairs. A chamois cloth smoothed over the coat helps remove static electricity and flatten the coat.

earned a championship in show already, and is whole (not castrated or spayed), check the Novice space under Championship Division, or, if it has been castrated or spayed, the Novice space under Alter (Premier) Division.

• If you have a Siamese that was already shown to champion or grand champion and the title was "claimed" (validated), it should be entered as a Champion or a Grand.

• If it earned a title as a whole cat and then was altered, it must enter as an Alter (Premier) Novice.

Benching: Benching refers to the cage position assigned to your cat in the show hall. If your cat is being agented, but sure to write that your entry must be benched with (name of agent). A physically disabled person might ask to be benched at the end of a row and near the judging rings. Frequently, friends ask to be benched together so that they can help

A Day at a Show

Let us take a quick walk-through of a show day.

1. Check-in time is given on the confirmation sheet as 8:00–9:00 A.M. You and Sammi (in her carrier) arrive at the show hall at 8:15 A.M. Just inside is the entry clerk, who checks you and Sammi in and either gives or sells you a show catalog (an absolute must).

2. The clerk or another official will direct you to your cage among 200 or so cages, usually arranged in double rows. On her cage will be a card with her entry number; let's say it is #132.

3. You put Sammi, still in her carrier, under her cage while you put a mat and small bed on its floor, obtain a disposable pan with litter (usually provided by the show), and half fill her water dish.

4. Now Sammi gets transferred from her carrier to her cage. She will probably be nervous. Pull up a chair and say sweet nothings to her while you quickly check out the competition in the show catalog.

5. Turning to the page where Sammi is listed, you see that there is another lilac-point female novice, #133, who will be in direct competition with Sammi, as well as a lilac-point male novice, #131, and a lilac-point female grand champion, #134. So there will be four lilac points competing for the best of color in their color class.

These lilac-point kittens, bred at the San-Toi Cattery by Deanne Johnson and Connie Roberts, show different intensity of eye color. For showing, the darker shades are preferred. The kittens' body language (making themselves small) indicates apprehension.

In some registries, lynx points and other colors besides the basic four (seal, blue, lilac, and chocolate point) are accepted as Siamese. In others, they are considered a separate breed called the Colorpoint Shorthair.

6. On the back of the catalog will be a show schedule. Each judging ring is listed, with the order of judging under it. Circle Sammi's group—Championship, Siamese—for each ring

so that you will be able to tell at a glance where she will be called for judging throughout the day.

7. If Sammi has settled, take a walk around and see if you can spot cage #133. There she is. Hmmmm. Her coat is nice and flat, but her ears are too small, and is that a little scratch on her nose? Check on Sammi, and, if time permits, the other lilac points. By now, the show should be getting underway.

8. Check-in time is over, and the entry clerk announces that he is ready to read the absentees and transfers. When he gets to the Siamese numbers he says that #131 has been transferred to champion. Note this in the catalog. This means that since the lilac-point mate novice was entered in this show he attended another show and made his championship. Number 134 is absent, so put an A in the catalog by her number.

9. When the clerk is done with the absentees and transfers, the ring clerks will begin calling for the first groups to be judged in their rings. Sammi is near the beginning of the schedule for Ring 3, Judge Gamma, so keep your ears perked for Ring 3 announcements. Time to check her eyes for cruds, smooth her coat with a chamois cloth, and give her a little treat, such as four licks of baby-food chicken.

10. Then comes the fateful announcement, "Ring three wants the following cats: #131, #132, #133 . . . ." Put pen, catalog, and chamois in your pockets and holding Sammi close to you with both hands, carry her to Ring 3, and put her in the judging cage that has her number on it. Give her a gentle wipe with the chamois to settle her fur and your nerves, tell her not to be afraid, close the cage door, and find a seat in front of the judging table. The judge takes out one cat at a time, puts it on the table, scrutinizes it, returns it to its judging cage, writes in her book, and then may hang one or more ribbons on the front of the cage.

11. It's Sammi's turn. Will she behave? Will she let the judge stretch her out to see her body length? Will she cross her eyes? The suspense is indescribable. The whole world disappears except Sammi and Judge Gamma until she is back in the cage. Whew! No mishaps, but did she like her? The ribbons will tell, but first #133 must be judged. Her ears are definitely too small, but did Judge Gamma note this?

12. Ahhh, a blue ribbon for Sammi, and a Winner's ribbon, and a Best of Color! The clerk says they may go back. Honeybun! You were wonderful, you could make it to the finals! There are kisses and hugs for Sammi and another five licks of baby food at her cage.

13. At the end of the day, six or seven o'clock, Sammi has been through five rings, five judges, has won some and lost some, has had lots of licks of baby food, and it has been exhilarating. You gather up your ribbons and rosettes, put Sammi in her carrier, take down the cage drapes, and depart, a weary, happy, experienced exhibitor and Siamese.

Basis of Judging

These sorts of details are picked up readily. How the judges choose the best-of-breed Siamese and finalists takes a bit more study.

As a starting place, the consensus of standards from five registries has been constructed (page 87). This is not a substitute for the individual Siamese standards of the various registries, which should be obtained and studied if you plan to show.

General Siamese Breed Standard

The ideal Siamese is a lithe, fine-boned cat of medium size with long, tapering lines. Males may be larger than females. The musculature is hard and sleek. Coat color is restricted to the points (face, ears, feet/legs, and tail); eye color is blue.

Part	Points	Description
Head	20	The head is a triangular wedge, with straight lines from a finely pointed muzzle along the sides to the outer base of the ears, which are large and set so that they continue the side lines of the head when viewed from the front. Bulging masseter muscles (stud jowls) are allowed in males. Seen from the side, there is a straight line from the tip of the nose to the top of the head and another straight line from the nose tip to the chin, which should be neither jutting out nor receding. The distance between the eyes is no less than the width of one eye.
Eyes	10	The eyes are almond-shaped and set at a slant toward the nose and in harmony with the side lines of the head. The color is a deep, vivid blue.
Body	30	The neck is long and slender. The body is long and tubular from the shoulders to the hips and is firmly muscled all over. The legs are long and fine-boned, with the hind legs longer than the front. The feet are small and oval. The tail is slender and tapering. The length should be equal to the length of the body or of the extended hind leg. The cat appears hard, muscular, and bright-eyed. It is neither flabby, emaciated, nor fat. All of its parts should harmonize—for example, if the body is moderately long, the head should not be extremely long.
Coat	10	The coat is short, fine-textured, glossy, and close-lying
Color	30	The points are evenly colored and matched, well defined, and contain no white or ticked hairs. The body color is a paler, even shade of the point color. Older cats are allowed to have darker body shading, but there must be a definite contrast between the body and points.

100 points

Serious faults: Paw pads or nose leather of wrong color for points; miniaturization; sanded or shaved coat; crossed eyes; visible tail vertebral defects; white toes or spots.

Siamese are active, curious, fun-seeking cats that need plenty of toys to keep them occupied, perhaps a scratching post tree to climb for exercise, and most of all, a loving human companion to entertain. Always keep your camera handy, because your Siamese will provide plenty of memorable snapshots, as shown in these photos.

Books

Carlson, Delbert G., D.V.M., and Giffin, James M., M.D. *Cat Owner's Veterinary Handbook.* New York: Howell Book House, 1983.

Davis, Karen Leigh. *Fat Cat, Finicky Cat: A Pet Owner's Guide to Pet Food and Feline Nutrition.* Hauppauge, New York: Barron's Educational Series, Inc., 1997.

____. *The Cat Handbook.* Hauppauge, New York: Barron's Educational Series, Inc., 2000.

____. *Ragdoll Cats.* Hauppauge, New York: Barron's Educational Series, Inc., 1999.

Helgren, J. Anne. *Encyclopedia of Cat Breeds: A Complete Guide to the Domestic Cats of North America.* Hauppauge, New York: Barron's Educational Series, Inc., 1997.

Siegal, Mordecai and Cornell University. *The Cornell Book of Cats.* New York: Villard Books, 1989.

Whiteley, H. Ellen, D.V.M. *Understanding and Training Your Cat or Kitten.* New York: Crown Trade Paperbacks, 1994.

Magazines

Cats Magazine
Primedia Special Interests
260 Madison Avenue, 8th floor
New York, NY 10016
Web site: *http://www.catsmag.com*

Cat Fancy
Subscriptions:
P.O. Box 52864
Boulder, CO 80322-2864
(800) 365-4421
Editorial offices:
P.O. Box 6040
Mission Viejo, CA 92690

(949) 855-8822
Web site: *http://www.catfancy.com*

I Love Cats
450 Seventh Ave., Suite 1701
New York, NY 10123
(212) 244-2351
Web site: *http://www.iluvcats.com*

Pets Magazine
10 Gateway Blvd., Suite 490
North York, Ontario, Canada M3C 3T4
(416) 969-5488

CATsumer Report: The Consumer Newsletter for Cat People
P.O. Box 10069
Austin, TX 78766-1069
Web site: *http://www.prodogs.com/dmn/ gooddog*

Catnip: The Newsletter for Caring Cat Owners
Tufts University School of Veterinary Medicine
P.O. Box 420235
Palm Coast, FL 32142
(800) 829-0926

Cat Registries

American Association of Cat Enthusiasts (AACE)
P.O. Box 213
Pine Brook, NJ 07058
(973) 335-6717
Web site: *http://www.aaceinc.org*

American Cat Association (ACA)
8101 Katherine Avenue
Panorama City, CA 91402
(818) 781-5656

American Cat Fanciers Association (ACFA)
P.O. Box 1949
Nixa, MO 65714-1949
(417) 725-1530
Web site: *http://www.acfacat.com*

Canadian Cat Association (CCA)
289 Rutherford Road, S, #18
Brampton, Ontario
Canada L6W 3R9
(905) 459-1481
Web site: *http://www.cca-afc.com*

Cat Fanciers' Association (CFA)
1805 Atlantic Avenue
P.O. Box 1005
Manasquan, NJ 08736-0805
(732) 528-9797
Web site: *http://www.cfa.org*

Cat Fanciers' Federation (CFF)
Box 661
Gratis, OH 45330
(937) 787-9009
Web site: *http://www.cffinc.org*

National Cat Fanciers' Association (NCFA)
10215 West Mount Morris Road
Flushing, MI 48433
(810) 659-9517
Web site:
   http://www.nationalcatfanciersassociation.com

The International Cat Association (TICA)
P.O. Box 2684
Harlingen, TX 78551
(956) 428-8046
Web site: *http://www.tica.org/*

United Feline Organization (UFO)
5603 16th Street
Bradenton, FL 34207
(941) 753-8637
Web site:
   http://www.unitedfelineorganization.org

The Traditional Cat Association, Inc. (TCA)
P.O. Box 178
Heisson, WA 98622-0178
Web site: *http://www.traditionalcats.com*

Organizations and Web Sites of Interest

American Society for the Prevention of Cruelty
   to Animals (ASPCA)
424 East 92nd Street
New York, NY 10128
(212) 876-7700
Web site: *http://www.aspca.org*

Animal Poison Control Center
(888) 426-4435
(800) 548-2423
Web site: *http://www.aspca.org*

American Humane Society
P.O. Box 1266
Denver, CO 80201
(303) 695-0811
Web site: *http://www.americanhumane.org*

The Humane Society of the United States
   (HSUS)
2100 L Street, NW
Washington, DC 20037
(202) 452-1100
Web site: *http://www.hsus.org*

This seal lynx point kitten already has some tabby markings on the points, most noticeable on its tail.

Association of American Feed Control Officials
Web site: *http://www.aafco.org*

Siamese Internet Cat Club
Web site: *http://www.meezer.com*

Siamese Rescue Central
Web site: *http://www.siameserescue.org*

Siamese Cats
Web site: *http://www.siamesecats.org*

Animal Network, Pets in General
Web site: *http://www.petchannel.com*

The restriction of color to the extremities seen in Siamese is called "acromelanism."

This youngster shows the paler body color that is typical of the chocolate point.

top left: The large, slightly too round eyes of this blue cream point give it an especially appealing look.

top right: Providing your kitten with its own scratching pad or post will help save your furnishings from being clawed.

A sleek-looking lilac point.

Cover Photos

Norvia Behling: inside back cover; Jerry Bucsis and Barbara Somerville: front cover, back cover, inside front cover.

Photo Credits

Norvia Behling: 8, 9, 12, 13 (top), 16, 20 (top), 21 (top left), 24, 29, 32 (top and bottom right), 33 (bottom), 36, 40 (top and bottom), 41 (top right and bottom), 44, 45, 48, 56 (top and bottom), 57, 60, 61 (bottom), 64, 76 (top), 84, 92 (top right), and 93 (bottom); Jerry Bucsis and Barbara Somerville: 25, 73, 88 (top right), 89 (top left and top right), and 93 (top right); Richard Chanan: 21 (top right), 65, 74 (top and bottom), 89 (bottom left and bottom right), 92 (top left and bottom), and 93 (top left); Tara Darling: 13 (bottom), 17, 41 (top left), 49, 61 (top left), 68, and 85 (top); Gary Ellis: 4 and 61 (top right); Isabelle Francais: 2–3, 5, 20 (bottom), 32 (bottom left), 33 (top), 37, 53, 72, 76 (bottom), 80, and 88 (top left and bottom); Pets by Paulette: 28 and 52; Everett Webb: 81 and 85 (bottom).

Important Note

This pet owner's manual tells the reader how to buy and care for a Siamese cat. The author and publisher consider it important to point out that the advice given in this book is meant primarily for normally developed cats of excellent physical health and good character.

Anyone who adopts a fully grown cat should be aware that the animal has already formed its basic impressions of human beings. The new owner should watch the animal carefully, including its behavior toward humans, and should meet the previous owner.

Caution is further advised in the association of children with cats, in meeting with other cats, and in exercising the cat without proper safeguards.

Even well-behaved and carefully supervised cats sometimes do damage to someone else's property or cause accidents. It is therefore in the owner's interest to be adequately insured against such eventualities, and we strongly urge all cat owners to purchase a liability policy that covers their cat(s).

About the Author

Marjorie McCann Collier, a professor of biology, has bred and shown Siamese Cats for many years. She has been an all-breed judge for the Cat Fanciers' Federation, Inc. and has served as a guest judge in Canada and Europe. Karen Leigh Davis is a professional member of the Cat Writer's Association and is the author of *Compatible Cats, Fat Cat, Finicky Cat, The Cat Handbook,* and numerous breed-specific books.

All inquiries should be addressed to:
Barron's Educational Series, Inc.
250 Wireless Boulevard
Hauppauge, NY 11788
www.barronseduc.com

Library of Congress Control No. 2005050706

ISBN-13: 978-0-7641-2848-6
ISBN-10: 0-7641-2848-5

Library of Congress Cataloging-in-Publication Data
Collier, Marjorie McCann.
    Siamese cats : everything about acquisition, care, nutrition, behavior, and health / Marjorie McCann Collier and Karen L. Davis.
      p. cm. — (A Complete pet owner's manual)
    Includes bibliographical references (p.) and index.
    ISBN 0-7641-2848-5 (alk. paper)
    1. Siamese cat. I. Davis, Karen Leigh, 1953–
II. Title. III. Series.

SF449.S5C65 2006
636.8'25—dc22   2005050706

Printed in China
9 8 7 6 5 4 3 2